Happy Mother's Day 1990!
Love,
Joe, Lindy, Rick & Todd

Happy Mother's Day 1990!
Love,

The Great International Cookbook

The Great International Cookbook

With more than 200 Step-by-Step Recipes for
Seafood, Poultry, Meat, Vegetables,
and Desserts

International Culinary Society
New York

Note: an asterisk after an ingredient refers to the Basic Recipes section at the end of the book, where instructions or information about the ingredient or its preparation are given.

Contributors: Napo Faorenc, Antonio Piccinardi,
Savina Roggero, Donatella Volpi

Translated by Caroline Beamish, Elaine Hardy, Sara Harris

This 1988 edition published by International Culinary Society
distributed by Crown Publishers, Inc.
225 Park Avenue South
New York, New York 10003

ISBN 0-517-66952-8
hgfedcb

Printed and bound in Spain by Artes Graficas, Toledo
D. L. TO: 1216 -1989

Contents

Introduction

This collection of more than two hundred recipes consists of famous dishes from all over the world along with others that are creative, original and unique to this volume. There are elaborate recipes alongside others that take no time at all to prepare. All feature clear and detailed instructions, organized into step-by-step stages and often accompanied by a series of pictures illustrating the vital moments of preparation. All the recipes, therefore, from the simplest to the most complicated, are presented in a way that is easy to follow.

In the final chapter there is also an essential reference section—a selection of useful cooking tips ranging from advice on how to choose and cook certain foods, to basic recipes and suggestions on how to serve different dishes.

This book can therefore be of practical use to everybody: the skillful and experienced cook will have the possibility to create wonderfully delicious and unusual menus; those less expert can equally aspire to the creation of imaginative dishes, guided by the illustrations and instructions accompanying the recipes.

Appetizers

Scampi cocktail

Preparation: 30 minutes
(+ 1 hour for refrigeration)

20 scampi (Norway
   lobsters)
salt
1 cup mayonnaise
1½ tbsp ketchup
½ tsp Worcestershire
   sauce
2 tsp brandy
1 lettuce
parsley
1 lemon

1   Cook the scampi for 5
minutes in boiling salted
water. Drain, leave to cool
slightly, then shell.

2   Mix together the
mayonnaise, ketchup,
Worcestershire sauce, and
brandy.

3   Wash and dry the
lettuce and finely shred
the white part.

4   Mix the scampi with
the sauce, reserving a few
for the garnish.

5   Distribute the lettuce
between 4 stemmed
glasses, lining each with a
whole outer leaf.

6   Spoon the scampi
cocktail into each glass
and garnish with a slice of
lemon and a little parsley.
Refrigerate for 1 hour
before serving.

Salmon mousse

Preparation: 1 hour
(+ 5 hours for the mousse
to set)

14 oz fresh salmon, in one
    piece
2¼ cups *court-bouillon**
2 level tbsp gelatin
3 tbsp dry sherry
2 tbsp lemon juice
salt and pepper
1 cup heavy cream
3 egg whites
2 tbsp oil
gherkins
1 lemon

1 Place the salmon in a
casserole; pour in the
court-bouillon, cover with
foil and bake in a
preheated oven at 350°F
for 20 minutes.

2 Leave the salmon to
cool slightly. Remove and
discard the skin and
bones. Cut into pieces and
place in a blender or food
processor. Dissolve the
gelatin over gentle heat in
½ cup *court-bouillon* and
pour into the blender.

3 Add the sherry, lemon
juice, and salt and pepper
and liquidize until smooth.

4 Whip the cream until
firm but not too stiff. Beat
the egg whites until stiff
and fold both into the
salmon mixture.

5 Brush the inside of a
large mold or individual
ramekins with oil, pour in
the mousse, and chill in
the refrigerator for at least
5 hours.

6 Turn the mousse out
onto a serving dish and
garnish with sliced
gherkins and lemon.

Seafood salad

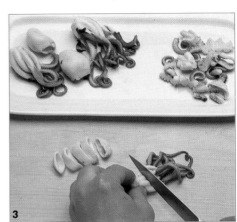

Preparation: 1 hour
(+ 1 hour for cleaning
mussels and razor clams)

6 baby octopuses, squid,
   or cuttlefish, cleaned
   (total weight 12 oz)
salt and pepper
1 celery stalk
8 oz mussels
11 oz razor clams
1 clove garlic
12 oz jumbo shrimp
1 bunch parsley
6 tbsp oil
½ lemon

1   Gently lower the baby
octopuses, tentacles first,
into boiling salted water.
Add the chopped celery
and cook for 8 minutes,
then drain.

2   Wash the mussels and
razor clams and leave
under running water for 1
hour. Drain, place in a
saucepan and sprinkle
with the chopped garlic.
Cover and cook gently for
4 minutes until the shells
open. Remove meat from
the shells and place in a
dish.

3   When the octopuses
have cooled, cut off the
tentacles and cut the
bodies into rings. Place in
the dish with the mussels
and razor clams.

4   Place the shrimp,
heads removed, in a small
saucepan with a little
water and salt. Cover and
cook for 4 minutes.

5   Peel the shrimp and
add to the other seafood.

6   Rinse and dry the
parsley. Chop finely and
sprinkle over the mixed
seafood. Season with oil,
lemon juice, salt, and
pepper. Stir well before
serving.

Salade niçoise

Preparation: 1 hour
(+ 30 minutes for soaking
the anchovies)

2 oz salted or canned
   anchovies
salt
8 oz potatoes
8 oz green beans
2 hard-boiled eggs
8 oz tomatoes
1 lettuce
7 oz canned tuna
5 tbsp oil
3 tbsp vinegar
⅓ cup small black olives

1   Rinse the salted
anchovies under cold
running water; divide each
one in half, remove the
backbone and leave to
soak for 30 minutes.

2   Boil the potatoes in
their skins in salted water
for approximately 20
minutes. Leave to cool;
peel and slice thinly.

3   String the beans and
boil in salted water for
about 8 minutes. Drain
and leave to cool.

4   Cut each egg into four
and slice the tomatoes.

5   Rinse and dry the
lettuce leaves and cut into
shreds. Drain the tuna and
flake.

6   Prepare a vinaigrette
by beating together the
oil, vinegar, and a little salt.

7   Place the lettuce,
beans, and potatoes in a
bowl and dress with half
the vinaigrette. Toss well.

8   Arrange on a serving
platter and garnish with
the hard-boiled eggs,
tomatoes, anchovies, and
olives. Pour over the
remaining vinaigrette.

Sardines in "saòr"

Preparation: 1 hour
(+ 30 minutes for soaking
the raisins and 1 day for
marinating the sardines)

1¾ lb fresh sardines
4 tbsp flour
oil for deep frying
2 large onions
salt
½ cup white wine vinegar
1–2 tbsp seedless white
   raisins
¼ cup pine nuts
2 tbsp candied peel
½ cup sour cream

1   Clean the sardines,
remove the scales, and
rinse thoroughly.

2   Drain the sardines well
and coat lightly with flour.

3   Fry the sardines in
plenty of very hot oil.

4   When the sardines are
golden brown and
cooked, drain on paper
towels.

5   Slice the onions finely,
sprinkle with salt, and fry
in the remaining oil. Add
½ cup water and cook for
10 minutes. Pour in half
the vinegar and simmer
for a few minutes.

6   Place the sardines in a
shallow dish, pour over
the remaining vinegar,
and sprinkle with the
soaked and drained
seedless white raisins, the
pine nuts, and chopped
candied peel.

7   Sprinkle with the
onions and sour cream.
Cover and leave to stand
in a cool place—not in the
refrigerator—for 24 hours
before serving.

Rollmops

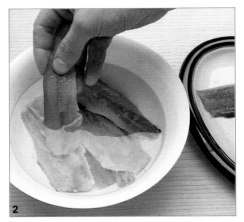

Preparation: 1 hour
(+ 4 hours for soaking and
3 days for marinating)

4 fresh herrings
½ cup salt
1¼ cups white wine
   vinegar
2 bay leaves
8 black peppercorns
1 tsp mixed spices
   (coriander, juniper
   berries, fresh dill)
2 onions
2 gherkins

1   Cut the head and tail
from the herrings; open
the fish flat and remove
the bones and entrails.

2   Dissolve the salt in 2¼
cups water in a bowl and
leave the herrings to soak
for at least 4 hours. Turn
them every 30 minutes.
Drain and dry the fillets.

3   Bring the vinegar to
a boil in a saucepan.
Add the bay leaf,
peppercorns, and spices,
remove from the heat and
leave to cool.

4   Slice one onion and
the gherkins and wrap
each fillet around a slice of
onion and gherkin.

5   Place the rolled fillets
in a glass or earthenware
jar and place the
remaining slices of onion
and gherkin between
them. Pour in the vinegar,
cover, and leave to
marinate in a cool place
for 3 to 4 days.

6   Slice the remaining
onion and serve raw with
the rollmops. Serve with
slices of brown bread or
rye bread and butter.

Soused herrings

Preparation: 40 minutes
(+ 12 hours for marinating
the herrings)

2 carrots
1 onion
1¼ cups white wine
1 cup wine vinegar
2 bay leaves
2 sprigs thyme
6 white peppercorns
3 cloves
salt
1¾ lb fresh herrings
1 tbsp parsley

1   Prepare the marinade:
finely chop the carrots and
onion. Place in a
saucepan with the wine,
wine vinegar, 1 bay leaf,
1 sprig thyme, the
peppercorns, cloves, and
a pinch of salt. Bring to a
boil and simmer gently for
10 minutes.

2   Clean the herrings:
remove the scales,
backbone, heads, and
tails. Wash and pat dry
with paper towels.

3   Place the herrings in a
flameproof casserole,
sprinkle with the chopped
parsley, 1 crumbled bay
leaf and a sprig of thyme.

4   Pour the marinade
over the herrings and cook
over moderate heat for 5
minutes.

5   Allow to cool, cover,
and refrigerate for 12
hours.

6   Remove from the
refrigerator at least 2 hours
before serving.

Herring salad

Preparation: 1 hour
(+ 24 hours for marinating the herrings)

4 salted herrings
2 potatoes
2 beetroot
1 cooking apple
1 cucumber
4 oz cooked veal
½ onion
2 tbsp oil
2 tbsp wine vinegar
salt and pepper
3 hard-boiled eggs
½ tbsp mustard
3 tbsp sour cream or plain
　　yogurt
1 tbsp chopped dill

1　Soak the herrings for 24 hours in cold water, changing the water as often as possible.

2　Boil and dice the potatoes. Dice the beetroot, apple, cucumber, and veal. Chop the onion. Cut the heads off the herrings; open the fish flat, pressing along the backbone; remove and discard the backbone and skin. Cut the fish into pieces.

3　Place all the ingredients in a large bowl and season with 1 tablespoon wine vinegar. Sprinkle with pepper.

4　Push the hard-boiled eggs through a fine sieve into a small bowl. Mix together 1 tablespoon wine vinegar, the mustard, and a pinch of salt. Stir in the oil gradually and add the sour cream last.

5　Pour the mixture over the herrings, stir carefully, and sprinkle with chopped dill and the sieved egg yolks. Cover and refrigerate for 3 hours. Garnish with hard-boiled eggs and lettuce.

Scallops à la provençale

Preparation: 20 minutes
(+ 1 hour for cleaning the
scallops)

2¼ lb scallops
salt and pepper
¼ cup butter
3 tbsp flour
2 shallots
1 tbsp oil
1 clove garlic
½ cup white wine
1 tbsp chopped parsley

1   Leave the scallops
under cold running water
for 1 hour; prize them
open and remove the
white meat and coral.
Reserve the shells. Discard
the black gristly parts. Cut
the white cushion in two
and sprinkle with salt and
pepper.

2   Heat 3 tablespoons
butter in a skillet. Lightly
coat the scallops in flour
and fry gently, a few at a
time, for 3 minutes until
golden brown. Cook the
corals for 1½ to 2 minutes
only.

3   Finely chop the
shallots and fry for 2
minutes in the remaining
butter and oil. Add the
garlic, cook for one
minute, then add to the
scallops. Pour in the wine.

4   Cook over moderate
heat for another 3 minutes.

5   Remove the scallops
and keep warm. Reduce
the sauce by boiling
vigorously.

6   Pour the sauce over
the scallops, sprinkle with
chopped parsley, and
serve in warmed shells.

Ceviche
(Marinated fillets of sole Peruvian style)

Preparation: 40 minutes
(+ 4 hours for marinating
the sole)

1¼ lb sole fillets
2 lemons
½ onion
1 clove garlic
few sprigs parsley
1–2 large ripe tomatoes
1 tsp chili powder
3 tbsp oil
salt

1   Place the fillets in a
deep dish and pour over
the lemon juice.
Refrigerate for 4 hours,
turning several times with
a wooden spoon. The fish
will turn white and harden.

2   Chop the onion,
garlic, and half of the
parsley very finely.

3   Peel the tomatoes,
remove the seeds, and
dice.

4   Mix together in a bowl
the onion, garlic, parsley,
tomatoes, chili powder,
and oil. Sprinkle with salt,
then turn these ingredients
into a serving dish.

5   Drain the fillets
(reserve the lemon juice),
cut into fairly large pieces
and arrange decoratively
on top of the seasoned
tomatoes.

6   Sprinkle with a little of
the reserved lemon juice
and garnish with parsley.

Deep-fried oysters

Preparation: 50 minutes

24 cleaned oysters
¾ cup milk
salt and pepper
6 tbsp flour
2 eggs
1 cup fine breadcrumbs

1   Rinse the oysters in cold water and drain well.

2   Place the oysters in a bowl and cover with the milk; leave to stand for 15 minutes.

3   Drain the oysters thoroughly and turn onto paper towels; pat dry all over.

4   Season with a little salt and freshly ground pepper.

5   Roll the oysters in the flour, coating each one thoroughly.

6   Beat the eggs in a bowl with a little salt and pepper and dip each oyster into this mixture.

7   Coat the oysters in the breadcrumbs, pressing the crumbs to adhere firmly to the oyster.

8   Heat the oil in a deep skillet or a wok; when the oil is very hot lower the oysters in carefully and fry until golden brown. Drain well and serve at once, garnished with lemon wedges, shredded lettuce and fresh parsley.

Spring rolls

Serves 6–12

½ cup lean pork or
   chicken, shredded
2 tbsp cornstarch
2 tbsp peanut oil
⅓ cup bamboo shoots
2 Chinese mushrooms,
   sliced
1 small leek, chopped
flour
12 Chinese pancakes*

For the sauce:
1 tbsp sugar
pinch of salt
½ tbsp soy sauce
2 tsp light soy sauce
2 tbsp chicken stock
1 tbsp peanut oil
few drops sesame oil
1 tbsp flour

1   Coat the meat with the cornstarch.

2   Heat the peanut oil in a wok and stir-fry the meat, bamboo shoots, and mushrooms for 1 minute. Add the sauce ingredients and stir-fry until the liquid evaporates; add the leek. Transfer to a plate and cool.

3   Prepare a paste by mixing 1 tablespoon flour with 1 tablespoon cold water and 2–3 tablespoons boiling water.

4   Place some of the filling along one half of each pancake; fold it over the filling, tuck in the edges, and roll up, sealing with the paste. Deep-fry the rolls in hot oil (350°F).

Terrine of pork

Preparation: 1 hour

1⅓ cups chopped pork
1 boneless chicken breast,
    diced
¼ cup shredded bacon
1 large onion
2 cloves garlic
1 bay leaf
¾ cup dry white wine
scant ¾ cup stock made
    with a bouillon cube
2 tbsp butter
few sprigs parsley
1 pitted black olive
pinch paprika
salt and pepper

1   Peel the onion and chop finely.

2   Shred the bacon, using a very sharp knife.

3   Melt the butter and add the onion, the finely chopped garlic and the bay leaf and sauté gently.

4   Add the shredded bacon and the chopped pork and sauté briskly over higher heat. Add a generous pinch of paprika. Pour in the wine and cook until it has completely evaporated.

5   Add the stock and the diced breast of chicken and leave to simmer over moderate heat until the meat is cooked through.

6   Allow the mixture to cool a little before placing in the electric blender or food processor; blend until the mixture is smooth.

7   Transfer the mixture to a bowl, season with salt and pepper and stir well.

8   Place the bowl in the refrigerator and chill for a few hours. Just before serving transfer to an earthenware dish or terrine, press down firmly and make a ribbed pattern on the surface with the tines of a fork. Place a black olive in the center and surround with a few flat parsley leaves or watercress.

Foie gras truffé en gelée

Preparation: 1 hour
(+ 3 hours for soaking the truffle)

1 large raw goose liver
1 truffle
2 large thin slices fresh
    pork fat
½ cup brandy
½ cup port
2 pints cold stock
1 pint chicken aspic
salt and pepper

For the chicken aspic:
½ lb chicken wings
1 onion
1 celery stalk
1 tbsp gelatin powder
2 pints water

1 Wash the truffle and scrape off the rough skin with a small sharp knife or brush. Place in a small bowl.

2 Pour the port over the truffle, followed by the brandy, and season very lightly with a pinch of salt and a little freshly ground pepper. Leave to soak for 3 hours. *To prepare the chicken aspic:* Make chicken stock with the chicken trimmings, vegetables and the water, boiling gently until the liquid has reduced to 1 pint strained volume. Dissolve the gelatin in this (do not allow to boil again).

3 Make a small, deep incision all the way to the center of the liver and push the drained truffle into this pocket.

4 Wrap the slices of pork fat around the liver, tying with string.

5 Wrap the barded liver in cheesecloth and sew up securely with thread.

6 Place the liver in the cold stock and bring to a gentle boil; simmer gently for 20 minutes.

7 Turn off the heat and leave the liver to cool gradually in the cooking liquid; when it is cold, take up and unwrap, removing the fat.

8 Pour some of the chicken aspic into an oblong or oval terrine; cover and chill in the refrigerator until just set; place the sliced goose liver on top and cover with more aspic. Return to the refrigerator to set. Chop the remaining chilled aspic and use to garnish the dish.

Hsao mai

(Chinese steamed dumplings)

For the filling:
¾ lb onions
½ cup cornstarch
1¾ cups ground lean pork
20 *hsao mai* dough
    sheets*

Seasonings:
2 tbsp rice wine
½ tsp salt
½ tsp sugar
1 tbsp soy sauce
1 tbsp sesame oil
pinch pepper
½ tsp chopped root
    ginger

For the toppings:
2–3 egg yolks
peanut oil
seaweed as required
3 slices cooked ham
1 small can crab meat
3 Chinese aromatic
    mushrooms (*tung ku*
    variety)

1   To prepare the scrambled eggs for the topping, heat a little peanut oil in a wok, pour in the beaten egg yolks, and cook over gentle heat, breaking up the egg yolks as they set.

2   Prepare the filling: chop the onions finely, add the cornstarch and mix well.

3   Mix all the seasonings together. Place the ground pork in a bowl, add the seasoning mixture, and mix well until smooth.

4   Add the floured onion to the meat mixture; mix well.

5   Make a loose fist, thumb upward, with one hand, stretch a dumpling sheet over the hole formed by thumb and forefinger. Place some filling in the center of the dough sheet and push down into the hole, supporting the bottom of the little bag with the little finger of the same hand.

6   When all the dough sheets are filled in this way, decorate the tops with a selection of chopped seaweed, chopped ham, scrambled egg, chopped crab meat, and the dried Chinese mushrooms (previously soaked in warm water for 30 minutes and chopped).

7   Brush the bottom of a bamboo steamer with a thin film of oil, arrange the *hsao mai* carefully in the steamer and place over boiling water. Cover and steam for 9 to 12 minutes.

Pasta, Rice, and Cereals

Chilled spaghettini with caviar

Preparation: 20 minutes

8 oz spaghettini
salt
4 tbsp olive oil
1 tbsp chopped fresh
  chives
4 tbsp caviar

1   Cook the spaghettini
in boiling salted water for
8–10 minutes until *al
dente*. Drain.

2   Leave to stand under
cold running water in a
colander for at least 1
minute.

3   Pour into a large bowl,
add the olive oil and
chopped chives and mix
well.

4   Serve in individual
dishes, each portion
garnished with a spoonful
of caviar.

Spaghettini with tomato sauce

Preparation: 30 minutes

12 oz spaghettini
½ onion
1 clove garlic
8 tbsp olive oil
14 oz ripe tomatoes
salt
black pepper
1 tbsp chopped fresh basil
fresh basil leaves

1   Mince the onion and garlic and fry briefly in the olive oil in a skillet.

2   Skin and seed the tomatoes and cut into strips. Sprinkle with salt and add to the onions. Cover and cook gently for 5–8 minutes.

3   Cook the spaghettini in a large saucepan of boiling salted water for 8–10 minutes until *al dente*. Drain.

4   Pour the spaghettini into the sauce; sprinkle with freshly ground black pepper, stir well and add the chopped basil.

5   Serve in heated dishes and garnish with the whole basil leaves.

Seafood spaghettini

Preparation: 50 minutes
(+ 2 hours to clean the
molluscs)

8 oz spaghettini
2 lb assorted molluscs
  (mussels, clams, sea
  dates)
4 jumbo shrimp
salt
6 tbsp olive oil
1 ripe tomato
1 clove garlic
1 tbsp chopped fresh
  parsley
black pepper

1   Leave the molluscs to
stand in a colander under
cold running water for 2
hours to remove all traces
of sand. Drain and place in
a large skillet. Cover and
heat for 3 minutes until the
shells open.

2   Remove the meat from
the shells. Reserve and
strain the cooking liquor.

3   Steam the jumbo
shrimp or cook in salted
water for 4 minutes.

4   Pour 5 tbsp olive oil
into a large skillet. Skin,
seed and chop the tomato
and add to the oil. Cook
for 5 minutes then add the
molluscs, shrimp and
reserved liquor.

5   Pour 1 tbsp oil into a
small skillet, add the
minced garlic and cook
over low heat for 2
minutes.

6   Cook the spaghettini
in boiling salted water for
8–10 minutes until *al
dente*. Drain and pour into
the skillet with the tomato
sauce and molluscs.
Sprinkle with freshly
ground black pepper,
chopped parsley and the
garlic-flavored oil. Mix
well before serving.

Spaghetti alla carbonara

Preparation: 30 minutes

10 oz spaghetti
4 oz pancetta or bacon
1 tbsp olive oil
1 clove garlic
2 eggs
salt
black pepper
2 tbsp grated Pecorino
   cheese
2 tbsp grated Parmesan

1   Cut the bacon into small dice.

2   Heat the olive oil in a small saucepan, add the minced garlic and bacon and brown gently for 3 minutes. Discard the garlic.

3   Cook the spaghetti in boiling salted water for 10–12 minutes until *al dente*. Drain.

4   Beat together the eggs, salt, freshly ground black pepper and grated cheeses and pour into a very hot soup tureen.

5   Pour the spaghetti into the tureen.

6   Add the browned bacon and any remaining oil. Stir well before serving.

Spaghettini with garlic, oil and chili pepper

Preparation: 20 minutes

12 oz spaghettini
4 cloves garlic
¾ cup olive oil
½ red chili pepper
salt
1 tbsp chopped fresh
    parsley

1   Skin and finely dice the cloves of garlic. Place in a large skillet with the olive oil.

2   Cut the chili pepper into very fine rings, discarding the seeds, and add to the skillet with the garlic. Fry very gently for 2 minutes.

3   Cook the spaghettini in boiling salted water for 8–10 minutes until *al dente*.

4   Drain and pour into the skillet. Add the chopped parsley and mix well for 2 minutes over heat before serving.

Bucatini all'amatriciana

Preparation: 30 minutes

12 oz bucatini
4 oz pancetta or bacon
10 oz ripe tomatoes
3 tbsp olive oil
salt
½ clove garlic
2 leaves fresh basil
½ red chili pepper
3 tbsp grated Parmesan
3 tbsp grated mature
   Pecorino cheese

1   Cut the rind off the pancetta and cut into ¼ × 1½-in strips.

2   Prepare the tomato sauce: Skin, seed and coarsely chop the tomatoes. Heat in a skillet for 10 minutes with the olive oil, a little salt and the garlic. Add the basil and cook for a further 5 minutes.

3   Remove the garlic and basil and sieve the tomatoes.

4   Gently brown the pancetta in no extra oil with the minced chili pepper.

5   Cook the bucatini in plenty of boiling salted water for 10–12 minutes until *al dente*. Drain.

6   Pour the bucatini into a heated serving dish. Sprinkle with the pancetta and any fat in the skillet, the tomato sauce and grated cheeses. Stir, cover and leave to stand for 3 minutes before serving.

Bucatini with broccoli

Preparation: 30 minutes

10 oz bucatini
1¾ lb broccoli
salt
8 tbsp olive oil
¼ red chili pepper
1 clove garlic
2 oz salted anchovies

1   Rinse and trim the broccoli, keeping only the tops.

2   Cook them in boiling salted water for 8–10 minutes until tender but still crisp. Drain, reserving the water, and keep warm.

3   Cook the bucatini in the reserved water for 10–12 minutes.

4   When almost *al dente* return the broccoli to the water. Drain after 2 minutes.

5   Pour the olive oil into a large skillet. Add the chopped chili pepper, the finely diced garlic and the rinsed, boned and chopped anchovies.

6   Heat for 3 minutes then add the bucatini and broccoli. Stir gently for 1 minute then serve. Sprinkle with grated Parmesan if desired.

Fettuccine with ham and cream cheese

Preparation: 20 minutes

12 oz fettuccine
salt
3 oz cooked ham, in one
  slice
½ cup mascarpone
  (cream cheese)
2–3 tbsp grated Parmesan
black pepper

1   Cook the fettuccine in boiling salted water for 6 minutes until *al dente*. Drain.

2   Cut the ham into thin strips. Heat for a few minutes in a saucepan with 1 tbsp cream cheese.

3   Mix together the remaining cream cheese, Parmesan and a little freshly ground black pepper in a warm serving dish and stir well.

4   Add the piping hot fettuccine and the strips of ham. Stir well and serve.

Penne with peppers and zucchini

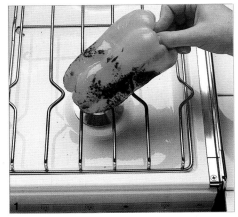

Preparation: 30 minutes

10 oz fluted penne
1 sweet yellow pepper
2 small zucchini
3 tbsp butter
salt
8 oz freshly made tomato
   sauce*
4 zucchini flowers
¼ cup flour
⅔ cup vegetable oil
1 tbsp chopped fresh
   parsley
black pepper

1 Scorch the pepper over high heat until the skin blisters, then rub the skin off.

2 Skin the zucchini and cut them and the pepper into small dice.

3 Melt the butter in a large skillet; add the diced pepper and fry for 5 minutes. Add the zucchini, sprinkle with salt and fry until the vegetables are tender but still crisp. Stir in the tomato sauce.

4 Dip the zucchini flowers in flour and fry briefly in vegetable oil. Drain. Sprinkle with salt.

5 Cook the penne in plenty of boiling salted water for 10–12 minutes until *al dente*.

6 Drain and add to the skillet with the vegetables. Stir and sprinkle with chopped parsley and freshly ground black pepper. Garnish each serving with a fried zucchini flower.

Penne with black olives and tomatoes

Preparation: 30 minutes

10 oz penne
12 oz ripe tomatoes
6 tbsp olive oil
salt
⅔ cup black olives
½ tsp oregano
1 tbsp grated Pecorino
   cheese
black pepper
4 leaves fresh basil

1   Skin the tomatoes and discard the seeds.

2   Chop coarsely and heat in the olive oil in a large skillet. Sprinkle with salt.

3   After 6 minutes, add the pitted olives and the oregano. Cook for a further 5 minutes.

4   Cook the penne in boiling salted water for 10—12 minutes until *al dente*. Drain.

5   Add the penne to the tomatoes and olives. Sprinkle with the Pecorino and freshly ground black pepper and stir well over high heat for 2 minutes.

6   Turn into a heated serving dish and garnish with fresh basil.

Penne with clams and peas

Preparation: 40 minutes
(+ 2 hours to clean the clams)

10 oz fluted penne
14 oz clams
14 oz peas
6 tbsp olive oil
salt
1 tbsp chopped fresh
    parsley
black pepper

1   Leave the clams in a colander under cold running water for 2 hours to remove all traces of sand.

2   Drain and heat for 2–3 minutes in a large covered skillet over high heat until the shells open.

3   Remove the clams from their shells. Strain and reserve the cooking liquor.

4   Shell the peas and simmer for 12 minutes in a large skillet with the olive oil and ½ cup of the reserved liquor. Season with salt.

5   Cook the penne in boiling salted water for 10–12 minutes until *al dente*. Drain.

6   Add the clams to the peas and cook for a further 2 minutes. Add salt if necessary. Pour in the penne, sprinkle with chopped parsley and black pepper and mix well for 1 minute before serving.

Maltagliati with duck

Preparation: 2 hours

12 oz maltagliati
1 young duck, cleaned,
    liver reserved
3 carrots
1 onion
1 celery stalk
1 tbsp chopped fresh
    parsley
1¾ cups red wine
salt
pepper
4 oz zucchini
1 tbsp olive oil
¼ cup butter
16 black olives, pitted

For the pasta:
2 cups flour
2 eggs
1 egg yolk
salt

1   Prepare the pasta dough* by mixing together the flour, eggs, salt and a little water. Roll out in a thin sheet and cut into rectangles, then triangles, using a sharp knife.

2   Using a sharp knife, carefully cut away the breast fillets from the duck.

3   Roughly chop the rest of the carcass into pieces and place in a saucepan with one carrot, the onion, celery and chopped parsley. Add the red wine and simmer for about 15 minutes until slightly reduced.

4   Strain the stock and adjust the seasoning. Add the crushed reserved duck liver and cook for a few more minutes.

5   Cut the zucchini and remaining carrots into thin strips and blanch in boiling salted water for a couple of minutes.

6   Brown the duck breast fillets briefly in the olive oil; sprinkle with salt and pepper and cook for a few minutes so that the meat is still pink.

7   Leave to cool slightly then cut into small pieces.

8   Cook the maltagliati in boiling salted water for 2–3 minutes only, then drain. Put the sauce, butter, vegetables, sliced duck, halved olives and drained maltagliati into a large skillet. Season with salt and pepper and stir well before serving.

Country-style macaroni

Preparation: 20 minutes

10 oz macaroni
salt
3 egg yolks
6 tbsp grated Parmesan
⅔ cup mascarpone
   (cream cheese)
black pepper
nutmeg

1   Cook the macaroni in boiling salted water for 10–12 minutes until *al dente*. Drain.

2   Mix the egg yolks with the grated Parmesan in a large, very hot tureen.

3   Place the tureen over a saucepan of boiling water so that it is heated by the steam.

4   Add the mascarpone, a generous sprinkling of freshly ground black pepper and a pinch of nutmeg. Stir well.

5   Pour in the very hot macaroni and mix well over heat before serving.

Macaroni with four cheeses

Preparation: 30 minutes

10 oz macaroni
salt
2 oz Gorgonzola cheese
1½ oz Fontina cheese
1½ oz Emmenthal cheese
2 tbsp butter
4 tbsp grated Parmesan
black pepper

1   Cook the macaroni in boiling salted water for 10–12 minutes until *al dente.*

2   Drain well and transfer to a buttered flameproof pan.

3   Dice the cheeses and sprinkle evenly over the top.

4   Place in a preheated oven, at 325°F, for 6 minutes.

5   Remove from the oven, add the butter and sprinkle with the grated Parmesan and plenty of freshly ground black pepper. Stir well for 2 minutes over high heat before serving.

Macaroni with fresh sardines and dill

Preparation: 1 hour
(+ 30 minutes for soaking
the raisins)

2–3 tbsp seedless white
   raisins
4 oz fresh dill
salt and pepper
12 oz fresh sardines
1 large onion
6 tbsp oil
3 tomatoes
¼ cup pine nuts
4 anchovy fillets
9 oz macaroni

1 Soak the seedless
white raisins in warm
water for 30 minutes. Trim
and wash the dill weed,
reserving the feathery
green leaves. Cook the dill
weed in plenty of salted
water for 10 minutes.
Drain well, reserving the
water, and chop.

2 Clean and rinse the
sardines; cut off the heads,
open out flat, and pat dry
with paper towels.

3 Fry the finely chopped
onion in the oil for 5
minutes in a large skillet.
Add the seeded and
chopped tomatoes, pine
nuts, and drained raisins.

4 Cook for a further 5
minutes, then add the
sardines and chopped dill.
Season with salt and
pepper, cover, and
simmer for 10 minutes.

5 Add the finely
chopped anchovy fillets
and cook for another 5
minutes.

6 Bring the reserved
cooking water to a boil
and cook the macaroni for
10 to 12 minutes or until *al
dente*. Drain well and mix
gently with the sardine,
anchovy, and tomato
mixture.

Pasta spirals with mussels and potatoes

Preparation: 40 minutes
(+ 2 hours to clean the mussels)

8 oz pasta spirals
1 lb mussels
8 oz potatoes
salt
½ cup olive oil
pepper
1 tbsp chopped fresh
   parsley

1   Leave the mussels for 2 hours under cold running water.

2   Drain well and place in a large covered skillet over high heat for 3 minutes until the shells open.

3   Remove the mussels from their shells. Discard any that do not open. Strain and reserve the liquor.

4   Peel and slice the potatoes and cut into pieces.

5   Boil in salted water for 5–8 minutes or until tender. Drain.

6   Heat the olive oil in a large skillet. Add the mussels and potatoes and cook for 2 minutes. Add 6 tbsp of the reserved liquor.

7   Cook the pasta spirals in boiling salted water for 10–12 minutes until *al dente.*

8   Drain and pour into the skillet; sprinkle with pepper and chopped parsley and stir before serving.

Trenette with pesto (basil sauce)

Preparation: 1 hour 10 minutes

10 oz trenette
4 oz potatoes
2 oz green beans
salt
8 tbsp pesto sauce*
2 tbsp grated Pecorino cheese

1   Skin, rinse and cut the potatoes into cubes. Rinse and slice the beans.

2   Cook the vegetables in boiling salted water until tender. Drain, reserving the cooking water, and keep hot.

3   Cook the trenette in the reserved water for 8–10 minutes or until *al dente*.

4   Drain and add to the vegetables. Stir in the pesto and grated cheese and mix well before serving.

Baked spinach lasagne

Preparation: 1 hour
20 minutes

10 oz spinach lasagne

For the meat sauce:
1 oz pancetta or bacon
1 tbsp onion
½ carrot
½ celery stalk
¼ cup + 2 tbsp butter
4 oz pork sausage
4 oz beef
2 oz ham
1 tbsp freshly made tomato
    sauce*
2 oz chicken livers
2–3 tbsp light cream
black pepper
1 cup grated Parmesan

For the white sauce:
3 tbsp butter
¼ cup + 3 tbsp flour
2¼ cups milk
white pepper

For the pasta:
2 cups flour
2 eggs, 1 egg yolk
½ cup cooked spinach

1 Mince the pancetta, onion, carrot and celery.

2 Brown gently in 3 tbsp butter, then add the ground pork sausage, beef and ham.

3 Cook for another 3 minutes, then add the tomato sauce diluted in a ladleful of hot water. Add salt and simmer gently for 40 minutes, adding more water if necessary.

4 Prepare the spinach lasagne*, combining the flour, eggs, a pinch of salt and the cooked and minced spinach. Roll out and cut into wide strips, then into squares.

5 Cook the lasagne for 3–5 minutes in plenty of boiling salted water (add 1 tbsp olive oil to prevent the pasta from sticking together). When they are *al dente*, drain and rinse with cold water to prevent further cooking. Place in a single layer on a clean teacloth to dry.

6 Prepare the white sauce: Melt the butter, add the flour and stir for 3 minutes. Stir in the hot milk gradually and cook for about 10 minutes. Season with salt and pepper.

7 Cut the chicken livers into small pieces and add to the meat sauce. Cook for 3 minutes, then stir in the cream. Simmer for 4 minutes, adjust the seasoning and sprinkle with a little freshly ground black pepper.

8 Butter an ovenproof pan and place a layer of lasagne in the bottom. Sprinkle with a little grated Parmesan, then with meat sauce, followed by white sauce. Repeat the procedure, making a second layer, then finish with a layer of lasagne. Cover with a thin layer of white sauce, sprinkle with Parmesan and a few flakes of butter. Bake in a preheated oven at 350°F for about 20 minutes.

Ham and cheese cannelloni

Preparation: 1 hour
10 minutes

1¼–1¾ lb cannelloni
salt
1 tbsp olive oil
3 tbsp butter
¼ cup + 3 tbsp flour
1¼ cups milk
white pepper

For the pasta:
2½ cups flour
3 eggs

For the filling:
1 cup ricotta
3 tbsp grated Parmesan
4 oz cooked ham
salt, black pepper

1 Prepare a sheet of pasta by combining the flour and eggs. Roll the dough out very thinly and cut into 4-in squares.

2 Cook in boiling salted water for 3–5 minutes with 1 tbsp olive oil to prevent them sticking. Drain carefully when *al dente* and spread out on a clean cloth.

3 Mix together in a bowl the ricotta, Parmesan, diced ham, salt and pepper.

4 Place some of the filling on each square and roll up into cannelloni.

5 Melt the butter and stir in the flour. Gradually add the hot milk, then simmer for 10 minutes, stirring occasionally. Season with salt and white pepper.

6 Place the cannelloni in a buttered ovenproof pan. Pour over the white sauce and place in a preheated oven, at 325°F, for 8 minutes before serving.

Tagliatelle au gratin

Preparation: 1 hour
10 minutes

14 oz green tagliatelle
¼ cup + 2 tbsp butter
¼ cup + 3 tbsp flour
1½ cups milk
salt
white pepper
6 tbsp grated Parmesan

For the pasta:
2½ cups flour
1 lb spinach
3 eggs
salt

1   Melt 3 tbsp butter in a saucepan. Stir in the flour and gradually add the hot milk; cook for 10 minutes, stirring constantly. Season with salt and white pepper.

2   Cook the tagliatelle* in boiling salted water for 3 minutes until *al dente.*

3   Butter an ovenproof pan and pour in one third of the tagliatelle. Cover with one third of the white sauce and Parmesan. Continue layering until all the ingredients are used up.

4   Place flakes of butter on top and bake in a preheated oven at 325°F for 8 minutes before serving.

Tagliatelle with sole and saffron

Preparation: 1 hour
10 minutes

10 oz fresh tagliatelle
10 oz sole fillet
¼ cup butter
4 fresh chives
salt
2 tbsp white wine
6 tbsp fumet*
pinch saffron threads
black pepper

For the pasta:
1¾ cups flour
2 eggs
salt

1   Rinse and dry the sole and cut into thin strips.

2   Melt half the butter in a large skillet. Add the chives and sole; sprinkle with salt, pour over the white wine, then cover and simmer for 4 minutes.

3   Heat the fumet and add the saffron threads.

4   Pour the fumet into the skillet and simmer for a further 2 minutes. Discard the chives, add the remaining butter and simmer for a further 2 minutes.

5   Cook the tagliatelle* in boiling salted water for 3 minutes until *al dente*. Drain.

6   Pour the tagliatelle into the skillet. Sprinkle with pepper and mix carefully before serving.

Pappardelle with partridge

Preparation: 1 hour
40 minutes (+ 6 hours for
the pasta to dry)

12 oz pappardelle
2 partridges
2 slices streaky bacon
2 sprigs rosemary
3 tbsp butter
1 tbsp olive oil
salt
black pepper
4 juniper berries
1 oz onion
½ celery stalk
⅔ cup white wine
2 oz truffle

For the pasta:
2 cups flour
2 eggs
1 egg yolk
salt

1   Prepare the pasta dough* by mixing together the flour, eggs and a pinch of salt. Roll into a thin sheet, cut into ¾-in-wide strips and leave to dry for at least 6 hours.

2   Clean, singe and rinse the partridges. Pat dry with kitchen paper.

3   Wrap a slice of bacon round each sprig of rosemary and place one inside each partridge.

4   Heat the butter and olive oil in a saucepan and brown the partridges on all sides. Season with salt and freshly ground black pepper.

5   Add the juniper berries, the chopped onion and celery and pour over the wine. As the wine evaporates add a few tablespoons of hot water or stock.

6   When the partridges are cooked, remove all the meat and shred. Keep the meat hot.

7   Break the carcasses with a cleaver and place in a saucepan with the cooking juices. Add 4 tbsp hot water and cook for 10 minutes. Strain through a fine sieve, reserving the stock.

8   Cook the pappardelle in boiling salted water for 4 minutes until *al dente*. Drain, then put in a saucepan with the reserved stock and meat. Stir well. Serve in individual dishes and sprinkle with slivers of truffle, thinly sliced with a mandoline cutter.

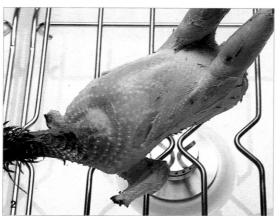

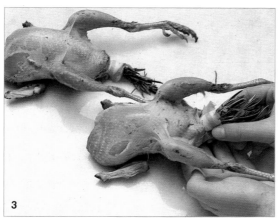

Tagliolini with chicken livers

Preparation: 30 minutes

10 oz egg tagliolini*
4 oz chicken livers
8 oz canned tomatoes
1 sprig rosemary
salt
pinch sugar
1 tbsp olive oil
3 tbsp butter
2 fresh sage leaves
pepper

1   Trim the fat from the livers.

2   Cut into ½-in pieces. Rinse under running water for 1 minute then dry well.

3   Purée the tomatoes in a blender and cook in a small saucepan for 7 minutes with the rosemary, salt, sugar and 1 tbsp olive oil.

4   Melt the butter in a large saucepan. Stir in the sage and chicken livers and cook for 2–3 minutes over low heat.

5   Cook the tagliolini in boiling salted water for 6 minutes or until *al dente*. Drain well.

6   Remove the rosemary from the hot tomato sauce. Pour the sauce over the chicken livers.

7   Place the saucepan over moderate heat, add the tagliolini, season with pepper and stir well before serving.

Tagliolini with mushrooms

Preparation: 1 hour

12 oz tagliolini*
12 oz *porcini* mushrooms
salt
½ cup olive oil
1 clove garlic
6 leaves fresh basil
1 tbsp chopped fresh
 parsley
1 tbsp grated Parmesan
black pepper

For the pasta:
2½ cups flour
3 eggs
salt

1   Wash the mushrooms in salted water; drain and then slice.

2   Heat 5 tbsp olive oil in a large skillet and gently fry the mushrooms for 5–8 minutes or until tender. Sprinkle with salt.

3   Cook the tagliolini* in plenty of boiling salted water for 3–4 minutes if freshly made, for 6 minutes if dried. Drain.

4   Brown the finely diced garlic in the remaining oil over low heat for 2 minutes.

5   Pour the tagliolini into the skillet containing the mushrooms, keeping the heat low. Add the garlic and oil, the minced basil and parsley and the grated Parmesan. Stir well, adding a little of the cooking water from the tagliolini if necessary. Sprinkle with freshly ground black pepper before serving.

Paella valenciana

Preparation: 1 hour
40 minutes

½ onion
1 green or yellow pepper
2 tomatoes
½ small chicken
4 oz pork tenderloin
½ cup oil
1 clove garlic
4 oz spicy sausage
salt and pepper
1 envelope saffron
   powder
1 bay leaf
2¼ cups stock or water
4 Norway lobsters
16 mussels

½ cup pilaf rice
4 oz shelled peas
pinch chili powder

1   Chop the onion. Char the pepper under the grill; plunge into cold water and rub off the skin. Discard the seeds and cut the pepper into thin strips. Peel the tomatoes, remove the seeds, and chop. Cut the chicken into pieces and dice the pork.

2   Heat 3 tablespoons oil in a skillet and brown the chicken and pork for 10 minutes. Remove and set aside. Put the sausage in the same skillet, prick with a fork and fry for 10 minutes. Set aside with the meat.

3   Add 2 tablespoons oil to the skillet and fry the onion and crushed garlic briefly. Remove the garlic as soon as it begins to brown. When the onion begins to brown add the tomatoes. Add salt to taste and cook for 10 minutes.

4   Place the scrubbed mussels in a saucepan, cover, and cook over high heat for 5 minutes until the shells open.

5   Place the chicken, pork, sausage, and bay leaf in another saucepan with 2¼ cups stock and simmer for 15 minutes.

6   Cook the Norway lobsters in boiling salted water for 3 minutes. Drain.

7   Heat 3 tablespoons oil in a large paella pan or cast-iron skillet and brown the rice, stirring with a wooden spoon. Gradually stir in the cooking liquid from the meat, the strips of pepper, and the shelled peas and cook for about 15 minutes or until the rice is tender. Dissolve the saffron in a little warm water and stir into the rice.

8   Stir in all the remaining ingredients. Mix well and place in a hot oven for 5 minutes before serving.

Fisherman's risotto

Preparation: 45 minutes

1¾ cups risotto rice
   (arborio)
½ lb squid
1 small onion
¾ cup oil
2–3 tbsp finely chopped
   parsley
2 pints fish stock*
3 tbsp tomato paste
1 green pepper
1 clove garlic
1 packet saffron
⅓ cup cooked peas
8 oz eel
12 clams
8 oz monkfish
8 peeled shrimp
salt and pepper

1   Wash and trim the
assorted fish; cut the squid
into rings.

2   Sauté the squid in the
oil in a heavy-bottomed
saucepan.

3   Add the finely
chopped onion and sauté
gently until it begins to
color.

4   Mix the tomato paste
with half a cup of hot
water and add to the
saucepan; add the eel
(skinned and cut into
pieces), the monkfish (only
the tail is used) and then
the shrimp.

5   Simmer for a few
minutes and then add the
rice.

6   Stir gently, adding the
hot fish stock a little at a
time, then add the seeded,
trimmed and diced green
pepper, the peas, clams,
saffron (dissolved in a little
stock), and finely chopped
garlic. Add a little salt and
freshly ground pepper to
taste. Simmer until the rice
is tender but still firm,
stirring frequently.
Sprinkle with the chopped
parsley and serve
immediately.

Risotto with quails

Preparation: 1 hour
15 minutes

8 quails
8 thin slices fresh pork fat
¼ cup butter
1 small celery stalk
few spoonfuls light stock
¾ cup brandy
3 tsp truffle paste
1 scallion
1 carrot
salt and pepper

For the risotto:
2 cups risotto rice (arborio)
3 tbsp butter
3 tbsp oil
1½ pints light stock
1 finely chopped onion
4 tbsp freshly grated
    Parmesan cheese
¾ cup dry white wine
salt

1   Wash and dry the quails; season inside each with a pinch of salt, freshly ground pepper and a little truffle paste and sprinkle with the brandy.

2   Truss each bird and wrap in a piece of pork fat, securing with cocktail sticks.

3   Heat the butter in a large, heavy-bottomed saucepan and fry the quails together with the finely chopped scallion, celery, and carrot.

4   Cook the quails over gentle heat for about 50 minutes, adding a few spoonfuls of stock to moisten every now and then.

5   To prepare the risotto: While the quails are cooking, heat 2 tablespoons of the butter and the oil in a deep skillet and sauté the finely chopped onion gently until it is a very pale golden brown.

6   Add the rice and stir well so that the grains absorb the flavors of the butter, oil, and onion. Pour in the white wine and stir until it has been absorbed or has evaporated.

7   Add about a cupful of boiling stock and continue cooking, adding more hot stock whenever it is needed. Make sure the rice does not stick to the bottom of the skillet. Add a little salt if necessary.

8   When the rice is tender but still firm and the risotto is very moist, turn off the heat and stir in the grated Parmesan cheese and the remaining butter. Transfer to a heated serving platter; remove the barding fat from the birds and place on top of the risotto. Pour the remaining cooking liquid over the quails and serve piping hot.

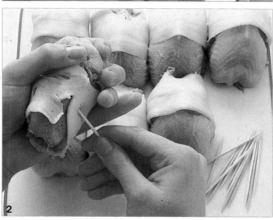

Rice with "caponata"

Preparation: 1 hour
30 minutes

4 eggplant
salt
2 medium onions
2 yellow peppers
4 zucchini
6 tomatoes
1⅛ cups olive oil
pepper
few leaves basil

¾ cup black and green
    olives
8 anchovy fillets in oil,
    chopped
1½ cups long-grain rice,
    cooked
½ lemon
1 clove garlic, minced
1 bunch parsley

1   Wash and trim the
eggplant; dice, place on a
clean tea towel and
sprinkle with salt. Leave to
stand for 30 minutes. Peel
and slice the onions, chop
the peppers and slice the
zucchini. Skin and chop
the tomatoes.

2   Fry the onions until
soft in half the oil in a
skillet. Add the eggplant
and peppers. After 10
minutes add the zucchini
and the tomatoes, skinned
and diced. Season and
simmer for 35–40
minutes. When cooked,
add the basil, pitted olives

and anchovies. Leave the
"caponata" to cool.

3   Dress the rice with oil,
salt and pepper and the
juice of ½ lemon. Add the
garlic, chopped parsley,
capers and a few basil
leaves. Arrange on a
serving dish with the
caponata in the middle.

Rice Spanish style

Preparation: 1 hour
30 minutes

1–1½ lb small chicken
¼ cup + 2 tbsp butter
½ cup olive oil
¼ cup brandy
salt and pepper
9 cups stock
¼ Savoy cabbage
2 carrots
1 leek
1 onion
1⅛ cups long-grain rice
3 egg yolks
2 tbsp soy sauce
2 tbsp chopped parsley

1 Brown the chicken evenly in a saucepan in 2 tbsp butter and 3 tbsp oil. Sprinkle with brandy and leave to evaporate. Add salt and pepper; cover and cook for 40 minutes, adding stock as necessary.

2 Cut the vegetables into thin strips. Fry the onion in 2 tbsp butter + 3 tbsp oil in a large saucepan. Add the vegetables and fry gently over low heat for 10 minutes, stirring occasionally. Season with salt and pepper; add 1⅛ cups stock and cook for about 25 minutes.

3 Bone the chicken and cut the meat into even pieces. Cook the rice in the stock until tender, then drain. Add the meat and rice to the vegetables, and stir.

4 Mix the egg yolks and soy sauce in a small bowl and pour over the other ingredients. Add the parsley and stir briefly over low heat until creamy.

Shrimp risotto

Preparation: 1 hour

14 oz shrimp
1 carrot
1 celery stalk
salt and pepper
½ onion
4 tbsp butter
2 tbsp oil
2½ cups risotto rice
   (arborio)
½ cup white wine
6 tbsp chopped parsley

1   Peel the shrimp.

2   Boil the heads and tails for 5 minutes in 5 ladles of water with the sliced carrot, celery, and a pinch of salt.

3   Crush the heads with a wooden spoon and pour the stock through a sieve.

4   Finely chop the onion. Melt half the butter in a saucepan and cook the onion, adding ½ cup water and a pinch of salt.

5   Melt the remaining butter in a skillet, add the oil and shrimp; sprinkle with salt and cook gently for 5 minutes.

6   When the onion is transparent, not brown, add the rice and the wine and stir over high heat for 2 minutes.

7   Once the rice is evenly coated, add the stock and cook over moderate heat, without stirring, until the rice is almost tender. Just before turning off the heat, add the shrimp and sprinkle with pepper. The risotto should be very moist.

8   Turn off the heat, add a little extra butter and the chopped parsley and mix well with a wooden spoon. Cover and leave to stand for at least 2 minutes before serving.

Rice sartù

Preparation: 2 hours

1 cup ground beef
3 eggs
8 tbsp grated Parmesan
breadcrumbs
salt and pepper
all-purpose flour
oil for frying
1 onion
1 oz mushrooms
4 oz sausage
2 cups frozen peas
2 tbsp tomato paste
6¼ cups stock
2 cups long-grain rice
2 tbsp butter
6 oz chicken livers
1 mozzarella

1   Mix together the ground beef, 1 egg, 4 tbsp grated Parmesan, 1 tbsp breadcrumbs. Season and shape into walnut-sized balls; dip in flour and fry for a few minutes in very hot oil. Chop the onion and fry in 3 tbsp oil. Add the mushrooms, the crumbled sausage and the peas. Stir in 2 tbsp tomato paste mixed with 2 ladles stock; season and simmer for 20 minutes.

2   Pour half the sauce into a saucepan; add the rice, then cook for 15 minutes, gradually adding the remaining stock (about 5½ cups).

3   Turn off the heat and add the remaining Parmesan and 2 eggs. Stir.

4   Butter a high-sided mold and sprinkle with breadcrumbs. Pour in three-quarters of the rice then press rice around the edges using a wooden spoon.

5   Fry the chicken livers for a few minutes in 2 tbsp butter. Add the meatballs to the remaining rice and fill the center of the mold with layers of sauce and meatballs, sliced mozzarella and fried chicken livers. Sprinkle each layer with a little grated cheese. Cover with the remaining rice. Cook at 325°F for 30 minutes. Unmold to serve.

Rice with anchovies

Preparation: 1 hour
(+ 30 minutes for soaking
the raisins)

½ cup basmati rice
salt
1 large onion
5 tbsp butter
1 tbsp seedless white
    raisins
Jamaica pepper
½ tsp powdered
    cinnamon
½ tsp sugar
1¾ lb fresh anchovies
1 tbsp pine nuts

1   Soak the rice for 30
minutes in warm salted
water. Soak the raisins in a
little water.

2   Finely slice the onion
and brown gently in half
the butter.

3   Drain the rice and add
to the onion. Fry for 5
minutes, stirring
constantly.

4   Add a ladle of hot
water, the drained raisins,
plenty of Jamaica pepper,
the cinnamon, sugar, and
salt. Cook for another 5
minutes.

5   Clean the anchovies,
remove the heads and
bones, and sprinkle with
salt.

6   Butter a large
ovenproof pan and cover
with a layer of anchovies.
Cover with the rice and
the remaining anchovies;
sprinkle with pine nuts,
dot with the remaining
butter and place in a
preheated oven at 350°F
for 10 minutes.

Fish soup with rice

Preparation: 1 hour
20 minutes

1 carrot
1 small onion
2¼ lb fish trimmings,
   preferably sole (heads,
   tails, bones)
1 bouquet garni
salt and pepper
¼ cup rice
2 eggs
juice of ¾ lemon
1 vegetable bouillon cube

1   Chop the carrot and onion and place in a saucepan with the fish trimmings and bouquet garni. Add 4¼ cups water and salt to taste. Cover and simmer gently for 10 minutes, stirring occasionally.

2   Add another 4¼ cups water and simmer for a further 20 minutes.

3   Strain the fish stock, pressing to obtain as much liquid as possible, and boil rapidly for 15 minutes to reduce.

4   Add the rice and cook for 15 minutes or until tender.

5   Beat together the eggs, lemon juice, and a ladle of stock in a bowl. Add salt and pepper.

6   Pour egg mixture into the soup and simmer gently for 3 minutes, stirring constantly. Do not allow to boil.

7   Remove from heat, cover, and leave to stand for 1 minute before serving.

Pilaf with lamb Turkish style

Serves 6

Preparation: 2 hours
(+ 2½ hours for soaking
the rice)

2½ lb leg of lamb, cut into
  cubes
pinch cinnamon
¾ cup butter
1 lb rice
2 pints boiling stock made
  with stock cubes
1 finely chopped onion
⅓ cup pine nuts
1 oz seedless white raisins
  (soaked)

6 large ripe skinned
  tomatoes (canned
  tomatoes may be used)
½ lb lamb's liver
1 tbsp finely chopped
  parsley
pinch sugar
salt and pepper

1   Wash the rice in a sieve under cold water, transfer to a bowl and cover with hot water; leave to stand for 2½ hours.

2   Sauté the lamb in a skillet for 15 minutes in scant ½ cup butter, until the pieces have browned evenly. Season with salt and transfer to an ovenproof casserole; place in a preheated oven (350°F) for 1½ hours, moistening occasionally with a few spoonfuls of hot stock.

3   Sauté the chopped onion in ¼ cup butter in a saucepan. Add the drained raisins and the pine nuts and continue cooking for a few minutes.

4   Crush the tomatoes with a fork. Add to the saucepan; pour in all the stock except for 1 scant cup and season with salt, pepper, a pinch of sugar and cinnamon.

5   Simmer for a few minutes and then add the soaked drained rice, cover tightly and place in the oven, still at 350°F, and cook until the rice is done.

6   While the rice is cooking, sauté the trimmed, washed and chopped liver in 3 tablespoons butter, add a pinch of salt and when the rice is done, mix in the liver and parsley. Spoon the rice pilaf into the center of a heated serving platter, arrange the cooked lamb around it and serve at once.

Jambalaya

Preparation: 50 minutes

1¼ cups long-grain rice
¾ lb shrimp, crayfish or
   scampi
1 cup diced ham
5 tbsp oil
¼ cup butter
1 clove garlic
½ onion
1 celery stalk
4 large ripe tomatoes

1 green pepper
1 bay leaf
1 clove
3 tbsp tomato paste
1 pint stock
1 cup dry white wine
oregano
salt and pepper

Jambalaya is typical of
Cajun cooking in
Louisiana. Rice is grown
in great quantities in that
area and the local
freshwater shrimp and
crayfish are highly prized.
The other ingredients may
vary, according to what is
in season.

1   The shrimp or crayfish should be raw and very fresh. Peel them and chop coarsely. (If only cooked shrimp are available, peel and heat only briefly.)

2   Heat the oil in a skillet and cook the chopped shellfish and diced ham over high heat for a few minutes. Remove from heat.

3   Chop the onion finely and sauté in 3 tablespoons butter until tender and transparent.

4   Add the washed and drained rice and cook over low heat for a few minutes, stirring and turning so that it absorbs the flavor of the butter and onion.

5   Stir in the shellfish and ham, together with the finely chopped celery and green pepper, the finely crumbled bay leaf, the clove, the peeled and crushed garlic, a pinch of oregano, and the peeled, seeded and coarsely chopped tomatoes.

6   Season with salt and freshly ground pepper and stir for a few minutes. Bring the stock to a boil separately; stir in the tomato paste and pour over the rice. Continue stirring and bring slowly to a boil.

7   Cook over low heat for 15 minutes. A few minutes before the rice is ready, add the white wine, mix well and then stir in the remaining butter. Cover the pan tightly with a lid, turn off the heat and leave to stand for 2 minutes. Heap the rice into a hot serving dish. Serve at once.

Rice with chicken and lobster

Preparation: 1 hour
25 minutes

1 2¾-lb roasting chicken
¾ lb fresh or canned
    lobster meat
2 green peppers
2 medium onions
4 large ripe tomatoes
¾ cup long-grain rice
1 cup oil
6 tsp soy sauce
pepper

1   Skin and bone the chicken and cut into strips.

2   Dice the lobster flesh (drain well if canned).

3   Pour ½ cup of oil into a large, heavy-bottomed saucepan and sauté the strips of chicken; add the diced lobster and continue cooking over low heat for up to 20 minutes.

4   Wash and dry the green peppers, remove the seeds and white membrane; peel the onions and chop these and the peppers coarsely. Dice the tomatoes and add to the peppers, onions and the remaining oil in another saucepan; cook over high heat for a few minutes.

5   Sprinkle the rice into the saucepan with the vegetables and continue cooking, stirring constantly, for 5 minutes more.

6   Add the rice, tomato and pepper mixture to the pan containing the pieces of chicken and lobster.

7   Add the soy sauce and plenty of freshly ground pepper; stir well and add just enough warm water to cover the rice. Boil briskly for 10 minutes, until the rice is tender but still firm. Transfer to a preheated serving dish and serve with extra soy sauce.

Five-color fried rice

3 dried Chinese
  mushrooms
2 oz cooked ham
3½ oz pork
1 leek
2 eggs
3½ oz shrimp
salt
3 tbsp oil

2 tsp soy sauce
pinch pepper
4 tbsp lard or cooking fat
4 bowls (up to 1¾ lb)
  precooked rice,
  (preferably boiled 24
  hours in advance)
1–2 tbsp peas, precooked

1   Soak the mushrooms in warm water for 20 minutes, remove the stems, and cut the caps into ¼-inch squares. Dice the ham and pork to the same size; chop the leek finely. Shell the shrimp and chop into pieces ¼ inch thick.

2   Beat the eggs and season with salt. Heat 1 tablespoon oil in a wok; pour in the eggs and scramble, then set aside on a plate.

3   Wipe the wok and heat 2 tablespoons fresh oil; stir-fry the mushrooms gently over moderate heat until their full aroma is released.

4   Add the pork and stir-fry, stirring to keep the cubes from sticking to one another; when the pork has changed color, add the shrimp and the ham. Fry lightly.

5   Once the shrimp have changed color, if raw, or have heated through, if precooked, pour in 2 teaspoons soy sauce, trickling it down the inside of the wok; stir and turn, giving the soy sauce time to flavor the other ingredients, and then season with pepper. Remove ingredients from the wok and set aside.

6   Clean the wok, pour in 4 tablespoons oil and heat; stir-fry the leek to flavor the oil but do not allow it to brown.

7   Add the rice and stir-fry over moderate heat, stirring and turning continuously, taking care not to crush the rice grains. Season with ½ teaspoon salt.

8   When the rice is well mixed and coated with oil, add the reserved ingredients and stir-fry; add the scrambled egg and peas and mix once more before serving.

Semolina gnocchi

Preparation: 1 hour
(+ 2 hours for the
semolina to stand)

2¼ cups milk
¼ cup + 3 tbsp butter
salt
generous 1 cup fine
   semolina
4 tbsp grated Parmesan
1 tbsp grated Sbrinz
   cheese

1   Heat the milk in a
saucepan, add one third of
the butter and a pinch of
salt.

2   Bring to a boil then
gradually stir in the
semolina. Cook for
20 minutes, stirring
frequently.

3   Remove from the heat
and stir in 2 tbsp grated
Parmesan.

4   Pour the semolina into
a dampened shallow dish,
spreading it out evenly to
a thickness of about ¼ in.

5   Leave to cool for 2
hours then cut into circles
1½ in in diameter.

6   Arrange the gnocchi
slightly overlapping in a
buttered ovenproof pan
and sprinkle with the
remaining Parmesan.

7   Melt the remaining
butter and pour over the
gnocchi.

8   Cover with the grated
Sbrinz and transfer to a
very hot preheated oven,
at 400°F, for about 10
minutes until lightly
browned.

Gnocchi Parisian style

Preparation: 50 minutes

1 cup water
½ cup butter
salt
1¾ cups flour
4 eggs
nutmeg
⅔ cup Mornay sauce*

1   Bring the water and ¼ cup + 2 tbsp butter to a boil in a high-sided saucepan. Add a pinch of salt.

2   When the butter has completely melted, remove from the heat and gradually add the flour, stirring constantly. Leave to cool slightly.

3   Beat in the eggs one at a time and add a pinch of nutmeg.

4   Spoon the mixture into a pastry bag with a 1-in-diameter tube. Pipe gnocchi 1½ in long into a saucepan of boiling salted water and cook for 15 minutes. Drain.

5   Heat the remaining butter in a small saucepan until light brown. Pour over the gnocchi.

6   Transfer the gnocchi to a lightly buttered ovenproof pan; cover with Mornay sauce and place in a very hot preheated oven, at 400°F, for 10 minutes until the top is golden brown.

Meat couscous

Serves 8–10

Preparation: 2½ hours

1 2¾–3-lb fresh chicken, boned and cut into pieces
3–3½ lb mutton (neck and shoulder), boned and cut into cubes
1 cup chickpeas, presoaked and parboiled
8 ripe tomatoes
½ lb pumpkin flesh (rind and seeds removed)
6 medium onions, sliced
1 envelope saffron powder
⅓ seedless white raisins (presoaked in warm water)
3¼ cups coarse semolina
½ cup butter
2 cloves
pinch mixed spice
pinch chili powder
salt and pepper

1   Bring 2 quarts water to a boil in a large saucepan. Rub the chicken and mutton with salt and pepper and add to the boiling water with the onions, chili powder, mixed spice, cloves, a piece of butter and the chickpeas.

2   Pour the semolina onto a large shallow plate and sprinkle with a cup of salted water. Work it over so all is evenly moistened.

3   Continue to knead the semolina. If too damp, add a little more semolina.

4   Sieve the semolina once it has amalgamated into small pellets. Spread out on a clean teacloth. Dry in the oven, at 250°F with the door open.

5   Add the chopped tomatoes and pumpkin flesh to the ingredients that have been boiling.

6   Spread the teacloth with the semolina inside a metal colander. Fold over the edges and place over the boiling meat and vegetables. Cover tightly and steam for 30 minutes.

7   Turn the semolina onto a large plate and separate any pellets that have stuck together. Sprinkle with a little cold water, mix very gently and sprinkle again.

8   After about 2 hours, when the meat is tender, remove from heat and drop in the seedless white raisins tied up in a cheesecloth; add the saffron and return to the heat. Replace the semolina in the colander and steam for 5 more minutes. Spread on a heated serving platter, dot with butter and gradually sprinkle with the stock from the meat. Arrange the meat and vegetables on the semolina. Serve the remaining stock separately.

Fish couscous

Preparation: 2 hours
15 minutes

2¼ lb assorted fish
   (scorpionfish, gray
   mullet, gurnard or
   other)
1 onion
1 clove garlic
1 large ripe tomato
1¼ cups oil
1 tbsp parsley
1 bay leaf
salt and pepper
scant 1 cup couscous
pinch nutmeg
pinch cinnamon

1   Clean the fish, rinse well, and drain. Slice the onion finely. Chop the garlic. Peel the tomato, remove and discard the seeds, and chop coarsely.

2   Heat scant 1 cup oil in a large saucepan. Add the garlic, chopped parsley, bay leaf and finely sliced onion, and brown for 2 minutes. Add the tomato.

3   Place the fish in the saucepan, with the largest on the bottom. Pour over 6¼ cups water, season with salt and pepper, and simmer for 5 minutes.

4   Remove the fish and keep warm. Strain the stock and pour three quarters into the bottom of a couscous pan.

5   Place the couscous steamer on top of the pan. (In the absence of a special steamer use a colander lined with cheesecloth or foil.) Place the couscous inside, pour over the remaining oil, stir, and cover tightly to prevent steam escaping during cooking.

6   Place a weight on the lid and simmer gently for 20 minutes. During cooking the couscous will absorb the flavour of the fish stock.

7   Pour the couscous into a skillet, stir in some of the reserved stock, and leave to stand for 1 hour. Add more stock as the couscous expands and absorbs the liquid, and stir.

8   Arrange the couscous on a warm serving dish and pour over the cooking juices. Season with pepper, nutmeg, and cinnamon. Add salt if necessary. Place the fish fillets on top.

Fish and Seafood

Gray mullet Bulgarian style

Preparation: 40 minutes

2 gray mullet, total weight
   2¼ lb
salt and pepper
2 tbsp fresh dill
2 tbsp chopped parsley
½ cup brandy

1   Remove the scales from the fish; clean, rinse, and pat dry.

2   Sprinkle with salt and pepper.

3   Mix together the chopped dill and parsley.

4   Grill or broil the fish for about 20 minutes, turning frequently.

5   Place the fish in a large skillet and sprinkle with the chopped herbs.

6   Heat the brandy, pour over the fish, and flame. Serve at once.

Leghorn red mullet

Preparation: 1 hour

8 red mullet, total weight
   1¾ lb
4 tbsp flour
½ cup oil
1 celery stalk
2 cloves garlic
14 oz ripe tomatoes (or
   canned)
salt
black pepper
1 tbsp chopped parsley

1   Clean, rinse, and dry the fish and coat lightly in flour.

2   Heat 5 tbsp oil until very hot and fry the fish over high heat for 3 minutes on each side. Drain and keep warm.

3   Finely chop the celery and garlic and fry gently in a large saucepan for 3 minutes in the remaining oil.

4   Add the peeled and chopped tomatoes, salt, and pepper and cook uncovered for 15 minutes.

5   Pass the tomato sauce through a vegetable mill or liquidize briefly.

6   Return the fish to the saucepan, cover with the tomato sauce, and reheat gently for 15 minutes.

7   Arrange the fish on a warm serving dish, cover with the sauce, and sprinkle with chopped parsley. Serve immediately.

Tempura

(Japanese mixed fry)

Preparation: 2 hours

1 small spiny lobster
16 jumbo shrimp
1 sole
salt and pepper
6 tbsp soy sauce
6 tbsp saké
2 tsp sugar
2 tbsp fresh horseradish
1 tsp powdered ginger
4 scallops
1 green pepper
1 carrot
8 oz green beans
2 eggs
1¼ cups flour
oil for deep frying

1 Remove the meat from the spiny lobster shell. Shell and clean the shrimp, removing the heads.

2 Fillet the sole. Make a fish stock by placing the heads from the shrimp, the head of the spiny lobster—the latter cut into four—and the bones and trimmings from the sole into a small saucepan with 2 ladles of water and a little salt. Simmer for 15 minutes and then boil rapidly to reduce.

3 Pour the stock through a strainer with a fine mesh and leave to cool. Add the soy sauce, saké, and sugar. Stir well and pour into four individual bowls. Before serving sprinkle with the grated horseradish and ginger.

4 Cut the fillets of sole into long strips; clean and slice the scallops. Cut the meat from the spiny lobster into slices.

5 Wash the vegetables. Dice the pepper and carrot; string the beans and leave whole.

6 Beat two egg yolks with a ladle of cold water in a bowl and work in the flour using a whisk.

7 Dip the pieces of fish and vegetables in the batter before frying.

8 Heat enough oil in a large cast-iron skillet or wok and, keeping the temperature constant, deep fry the fish and vegetables in batches. Season with salt and pepper and serve very hot. Each person dips a selection of fried fish and vegetables into the soy sauce.

Tuna Charterhouse style

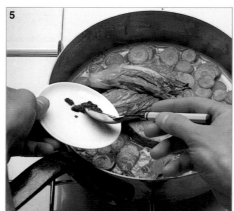

Preparation: 1 hour

4 tuna steaks
salt and pepper
1 lemon
4 anchovy fillets
1 onion
3 carrots
4 tbsp oil
4 lettuce hearts
1 bunch sorrel
scant 1 cup white wine

1   Place the tuna steaks in boiling salted water acidulated with the lemon juice and boil for 1 minute.

2   Drain and dry the tuna steaks. Make several incisions in each and insert the pieces of anchovy.

3   Finely slice the onion and cut the carrots into rounds. Pour the oil into a large saucepan, add the onion and carrots, season with salt and pepper, and fry for 4 minutes. Place the tuna steaks on top of the vegetables, cover and cook for 3 minutes. Add salt, turn the steaks, and cook for a further 3 minutes.

4   Cook the lettuce hearts in boiling salted water for 2 minutes.

5   Drain and squeeze the lettuce hearts and place on top of the tuna steaks. Rinse and dry the sorrel and place in the center of the steaks. Cook for 4 minutes over moderate heat.

6   Sprinkle with salt and pepper and white wine; cover and simmer for about 20 minutes. Serve each steak with a selection of the vegetables and garnish with a little fresh sorrel.

Conger eel Braganza style

Preparation: 1 hour

1¾ lb conger eel
½ cup oil
1 small onion
1 bay leaf
1 tbsp vinegar
salt and pepper
4 slices day-old bread
3 egg yolks
1 tbsp chopped parsley

1   Wash and dry the eel and cut into 2-inch slices.

2   Heat the oil in a saucepan, add the chopped onion, and fry gently for 5 minutes.

3   Add the eel, bay leaf, vinegar, generous 1 cup water, salt, and pepper. Bring to a boil and simmer for 10 minutes.

4   Arrange the slices of day-old bread on a heated serving dish and place the drained pieces of eel on top. Keep warm. Reserve the cooking liquid.

5   Beat together the egg yolks and parsley.

6   Stir the cooking juices gradually into the beaten egg yolks and parsley and heat gently until thickened. Pour the sauce over the eel and serve at once.

Sea bass with orange sauce

Preparation: 40 minutes

1 1¾-lb sea bass
6 tbsp oil
½ cup flour
salt
3 tbsp butter
scant 1 cup milk
3 oranges

1   Cut the sea bass into steaks ¾ inch thick.

2   Heat the oil in a skillet. Coat the steaks lightly in flour and fry for 10 minutes over medium heat, turning after 5 minutes. Season with salt, drain, and keep warm.

3   Melt the butter in a clean saucepan, stir in the flour and cook the *roux* for 2 minutes.

4   Stir in the milk gradually and cook for 5 minutes.

5   Squeeze two oranges.

6   Add the orange juice to the white sauce and cook for a further 5 minutes, stirring constantly. Add salt to taste.

7   Pour the sauce over the fish steaks and cook gently for another 5 minutes.

8   Wash the remaining orange and, without peeling, cut it into fine slices. Cut each slice in half and use for garnish.

Baked stuffed sea bass

Preparation: 1 hour

½ onion
½ green pepper
1 large tomato
6 tbsp butter
1 2¼-lb sea bass
1 tbsp chopped parsley
salt and pepper
½ cup white wine
fresh dill

1 Finely chop the onion and pepper.

2 Peel the tomato, remove the seeds, and chop coarsely.

3 Melt half the butter in a skillet and fry the onion, pepper, and tomato for 5 minutes.

4 Remove the scales from the sea bass. Make an opening in the side, clean, rinse well under running water and wipe dry.

5 Stuff the fish with the onion, pepper, tomato, and chopped parsley. Season with salt and pepper.

6 Sew up the opening carefully with kitchen thread.

7 Place the fish in a buttered baking pan. Pour over the wine and the remaining melted butter.

8 Bake in a preheated oven at 400°F for 20 minutes, basting frequently with the juices and sprinkling with chopped dill after 10 minutes.

Sea bream with olives

Preparation: 40 minutes

1 2¾-lb sea bream
6 tbsp oil
24 black olives, pitted
salt and pepper
scant 1 cup white wine
4 sprigs rosemary

1   Remove the scales, clean, and rinse the sea bream.

2   Pour the oil into a large skillet and fry the fish gently for 3 minutes on each side.

3   Add the pitted olives, season with salt, and pour in the wine. Cook for a further 15 minutes.

4   Add the sprigs of rosemary, sprinkle generously with pepper, and cook for another 5 minutes. Serve immediately.

John Dory with vegetables

Preparation: 45 minutes

1 2¼-lb John Dory fish
(porgy or scup, from the
Atlantic, may be
substituted)
2 tbsp flour
8 tbsp oil
salt
4 artichokes
sprig rosemary
juice of ½ lemon
1 cup white wine
1 tbsp chopped parsley
black pepper
2 tbsp butter

1   Clean and rinse the fish and cut into four. Wipe dry and coat lightly with flour.

2   Heat the oil in a large skillet and, when hot, place the pieces of fish in side by side.

3   Fry for 3 minutes on each side, then sprinkle with salt.

4   Trim the artichokes, discarding the tough outer leaves. Slice finely and add to the skillet together with the rosemary. Season with salt.

5   Pour in the lemon juice, add the wine, and cook for about 15 minutes.

6   Sprinkle with the finely chopped parsley and black pepper and cook, uncovered, for 3 minutes.

7   Arrange the artichokes on a heated serving dish and place the fish on top.

8   Make a beurre manié with the flour and butter; stir into the sauce to thicken, then pour over the fish.

Fried hake maître d'hôtel

Preparation: 40 minutes
(+ 2 hours for the *maître
d'hôtel* butter to chill)

8 small hake
2 eggs
flour for coating fish
2 cups fine breadcrumbs
6 tbsp white wine vinegar
oil for frying
salt and pepper

For the maître d'hôtel
  butter:
½ cup butter
juice of ½ lemon
1–2 tbsp finely chopped
  parsley

1   Work the butter until soft and then mix in the chopped parsley, followed by the lemon juice.

2   Roll the butter into a fat "sausage" in wax paper or foil (about 1¼ in in diameter). Chill in the refrigerator for at least 2 hours.

3   Gut the fish, wash well and dry.

4   Pour the vinegar into a bowl and dilute with an equal amount of cold water. Use a clean cloth wrapped around three fingers and dipped in this acidulated water to wipe the cavities of the fish; do not rinse off.

5   Coat the fish in flour and dip into the egg beaten with a little salt.

6   Roll in the breadcrumbs, pressing lightly so that the whole fish is coated.

7   Heat plenty of oil until very hot in a large skillet and lower the fish carefully into it.

8   Fry the fish until they are well browned, spooning hot oil over them occasionally. Remove and drain on paper towels. Slice the *maître d'hôtel* butter and place a round of butter on each fish. Garnish with sprigs of parsley and serve with steamed potatoes.

Skate au beurre noir

Preparation: 1 hour
(+ 2 hours for soaking the
skate)

2¾ lb wing of skate
salt and pepper
1 onion
2 carrots
4 sprigs parsley
¼ cup wine vinegar
10 peppercorns
1 bay leaf
1 tbsp chopped parsley
2 tbsp capers
6 tbsp butter

1 Buy ready-cleaned skate or have it cleaned and skinned by the fishmonger. Wash under cold running water and leave to soak in salted water for 2 hours.

2 Slice the onion and carrots.

3 Cut the skate into four.

4 Place the skate in a wide skillet with the onion, carrot, parsley, 3 tablespoons of wine vinegar, salt, peppercorns, and bay leaf. Cover with cold water, bring to a boil, and simmer very gently for 15 minutes.

5 Drain the skate and arrange on a serving dish.

6 Sprinkle with salt, pepper, chopped parsley, and crushed capers. Keep warm.

7 Melt the butter in a small saucepan and heat until it turns golden brown. Take care not to burn it. Pour the butter over the skate. Return the saucepan to the heat, warm the remaining wine vinegar, and pour over the fish. Serve immediately with boiled new potatoes topped with butter and parsley.

Turbot with scampi sauce

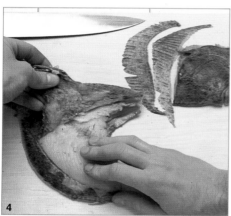

Preparation: 1 hour

3 Norway lobsters
½ tbsp flour
salt
6 tbsp butter
pinch mace
Cayenne pepper
1 2¾-lb turbot
scant 1 cup milk
½ lemon
pepper
1 tbsp chopped parsley

1   Boil the Norway lobsters for 3 minutes in 2 inches of water. Shell them, return the shells to the water, and cook for a further 15 minutes. Strain the stock and reduce by boiling vigorously.

2   Mix the flour with ½ cup of the stock and add a pinch of salt. Add the butter in pieces and cook, stirring constantly, for 3 minutes.

3   Add the meat from the Norway lobsters cut into pieces, a pinch of mace, and Cayenne pepper. Stir for 1 minute until the sauce thickens.

4   Clean the turbot: cut off the head and fins and remove the skin and entrails.

5   Cover with scant 1 cup water and the milk, then add the lemon juice. Season with salt and pepper and cook for about 15 minutes.

6   Drain the turbot, place on a warm serving dish, and sprinkle with chopped parsley. Serve with boiled potatoes and carrots and serve the scampi sauce separately in a sauce boat.

Salt cod Vicenza style

Preparation: 2 hours
(+ 2 days for soaking the
salt cod)

1¾ lb salt cod
2 onions
1 clove garlic
2 anchovies
1 tbsp parsley
salt and pepper
1 cup oil
½ cup grated Parmesan
2¼ cups milk

1   Beat the salt cod with a wooden rolling pin, then leave to soak in cold water for 2 days, changing the water frequently.

2   Cut the salt cod into strips 2 inches wide; open them out and remove the bones.

3   Skin each piece.

4   Finely chop the onions, garlic, anchovies, and parsley. Season with salt and pepper. Heat half the oil in a saucepan and fry the ingredients for 5 minutes before adding the Parmesan. Stir well.

5   Use the filling to sandwich the pieces of salt cod together.

6   Heat the remaining oil in a skillet, add the salt cod and any remaining filling.

7   Heat for 2 minutes, then pour in the milk.

8   Cook very gently for 1½ hours, shaking the skillet occasionally to prevent the salt cod from sticking. This dish is traditionally served with slices of fried polenta.

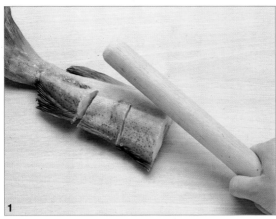

Steamed fish Cantonese style

1 whole very fresh
   nonoily, white fleshed
   fish, such as bass, carp,
   mullet, etc, weighing
   approximately 1¼ lb
2–3 dried Chinese
   mushrooms, presoaked
2 slices root ginger
2 slices ham
1 leek
1 tbsp rice wine
few drops of sesame oil
2 tbsp soy sauce

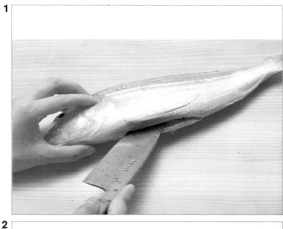

1   Always use the freshest fish for this recipe; gut and clean.

2   With a sharp knife remove the scales from the fish; wash it well in cold running water inside and out and pat dry.

3   Soak the Chinese mushrooms in water for 20 minutes, then drain. Remove the stems and slice the caps into thin strips about 1/8 inch wide.

4   Pound one slice of ginger with the blunt edge of the cleaver; cut the second slice into thin strips.

5   Shred the ham and cut the leek into two pieces, each 4 inches long.

6   Place the pounded slice of ginger in the cavity of the fish; lay the fish on its side in a heatproof pan with one piece of leek under its head and the other under its tail. Sprinkle the shredded ginger, ham and mushrooms over the top of the fish.

7   Moisten the fish with 1 tablespoon rice wine and a few drops of sesame oil for flavor; place the dish in the bamboo steamer, which should already be full of steam.

8   Steam the fish over rapidly boiling water for 15 to 20 minutes without opening the steamer; when the fish is done, remove the slice of ginger from the inside of the fish. Place the fish on a heated serving dish and sprinkle with the rice wine while still hot.

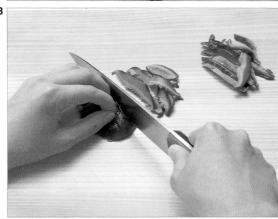

Mullet en papillote

Preparation: 1 hour

2 pompano, total weight
   2¼ lb
1¾ cups fumet*
1¼ cups dry white wine
6 tbsp butter
1 cup shrimp
1 tbsp parsley
2 onions
¼ cup + 3 tbsp flour
Cayenne pepper
salt
1–2 tbsp light cream
1 cup cooked crabmeat

1   Clean and fillet the fish. Rinse and pat dry.

2   Place the fillets in a skillet with half the fumet, the wine, and a little butter. Bring to a simmer and heat gently for 5 minutes.

3   Peel the shrimp and remove the central black vein. Wash and pat dry with paper towels.

4   Melt half the butter in another skillet, add the shrimp, and cook for 3 minutes. Sprinkle with chopped parsley.

5   Melt the remaining butter in a saucepan, add the chopped onions, and fry for 5 minutes; add the flour and stir constantly with a whisk for 1 minute.

6   Add the remaining fumet; bring to a boil, lower the heat, and simmer for 3 minutes. Stir in a little Cayenne pepper, salt, and the cream.

7   Cut out 8 foil heart shapes and butter 4 of them. Place a fillet of fish, a quarter of the shrimp, and a quarter of the crabmeat on each.

8   Spoon over a little of the sauce and cover with a piece of foil. Seal the edges well. Place the *papillotes* on a baking sheet in a preheated oven at 400°F for 8 minutes. Serve immediately.

Sole à la meunière

Preparation: 20 minutes

4 sole, total weight 2¼ lb
5 tbsp butter
2 tbsp flour
salt
1 tbsp lemon juice
1 tbsp chopped parsley

1   Clean the sole; remove the skin from the dark side and gently scrape the white side.

2   Melt half the butter in a large skillet. Dip the sole in flour and shake off the excess.

3   Gently fry the sole in the butter for 6 to 7 minutes, turning once with a fish slice, and season with salt.

4   When the sole are golden brown, transfer to a heated serving dish and sprinkle with a few drops of lemon juice and finely chopped parsley.

5   In the same skillet heat the remaining butter until golden brown and foaming. Pour over the sole and serve immediately.

Fillets of sole à la normande

Preparation: 50 minutes (+ 2 hours for cleaning the mussels)

1 lb mussels
scant ½ cup shrimp
1¼ cups fumet*
1½ cups mushrooms
¼ cup butter
4 fillets of sole (or 1 lb)
scant 1 cup white wine
salt and pepper
¼ cup flour
3 egg yolks
juice of 1 lemon

1 Heat the mussels in a covered saucepan for 3 minutes. Remove from the shells; strain and reserve the liquor. Heat the shrimp for 4 minutes in ¼ cup fumet. Peel them, place the shells in the fumet, and simmer for 5 minutes. Strain the fumet.

2 Wash and slice the mushrooms. Heat for 10 minutes in 1 tbsp butter.

3 Place the fillets in a buttered ovenproof pan with the wine and ½ cup fumet. Season. Cover with buttered foil and bake at 325°F for 8 minutes.

4 Pour the liquor into the remaining fumet and reduce over high heat.

5 Melt 2 tbsp butter, stir in the flour and cook for 1 minute. Add the fumet gradually and cook for 3 minutes. Beat the egg yolks and stir into the sauce. Add the remaining butter and lemon juice.

6 Transfer the fillets to another casserole. Surround with mushrooms, mussels and shrimp; cover with sauce and place in the oven preheated to 400°F for 5 minutes.

Spiny lobster Sardinian style

Preparation: 1 hour

2 1-lb spiny lobsters
2 onions
6 tbsp oil
1 tsp mustard
1 tsp vinegar
salt and pepper
2 medium tomatoes

1 Tie the spiny lobsters with string, plunge them into boiling salted water, and cook for 10 minutes.

2 Finely slice the onions and leave to soak in a cup of salted water for 10 minutes.

3 When the lobsters have cooled cut the tails in half.

4 Using a teaspoon carefully remove the creamy substance from the head and place in a bowl.

5 Add to it 5 tablespoons oil, the mustard, vinegar, salt and pepper, and stir vigorously.

6 Remove the meat from the tail and cut into slices.

7 Drain the onions, pour over the remaining oil, and chop the tomatoes into small pieces. Sprinkle with salt.

8 Arrange a layer of onion on each plate and place the slices of lobster on top. Pour over the sauce and sprinkle with the pieces of tomato.

Lobster Newburg

Preparation: 40 minutes

1 2¼-lb lobster or spiny
  lobster
salt and pepper
4 tbsp butter
½ cup Madeira or Marsala
2¼ cups cream
5 egg yolks
pinch Cayenne pepper
1 cup long-grain rice
2 tbsp chopped parsley

1   Tie the lobster with string and cook in a large pan of boiling salted water for about 15 minutes.

2   Leave to cool slightly, then remove the meat from the tail and cut into chunks.

3   Melt the butter in a skillet and heat the pieces of lobster for 2 minutes.

4   Pour in the Madeira and 1½ cups cream. Bring to a boil, lower the heat, and simmer for 2 minutes.

5   Mix the egg yolks with the remaining cream and a few tablespoons of the Madeira sauce.

6   Add the Madeira mixture to the skillet, stirring constantly. Heat gently until the sauce thickens but do not allow to boil.

7   Season with a pinch of Cayenne pepper, salt and black pepper.

8   Cook for a further 2 to 3 minutes. Serve on a bed of steamed rice and sprinkle with chopped parsley.

Lobster à l'américaine

Preparation: 1 hour

2 1-lb cooked lobsters
salt and pepper
scant ½ cup oil
½ onion
2 shallots
1 clove garlic
½ cup brandy
1⅛ cup white wine
4 ripe tomatoes
1 cup fumet*
pinch Cayenne pepper
1 tbsp tomato purée
2 tbsp parsley
1 tbsp tarragon
2 tbsp butter

1   Cut the lobsters in half lengthwise, removing and reserving the coral and liver, and cut each half tail into three and the head into two. Remove the claws. Season with salt and pepper. Heat the oil in a skillet, add the lobster pieces, including the claws, and fry over high heat, stirring until they turn red. Cook for a further 4 minutes.

2   Remove the pieces of lobster and add the chopped onions, shallots, and garlic. Fry gently for 8 minutes, return the lobster to the skillet, pour over the brandy and flame. Stir in the wine, chopped tomatoes, fumet, and Cayenne pepper. Cover and simmer for 5 minutes.

3   Remove the meat from the claws and tails and keep warm. Pound the shells and heads and return to the sauce. Add the tomato purée and cook for 5 minutes. Sieve the sauce and reduce over high heat. Stir in the coral and liver, the parsley and tarragon, and the pieces of lobster. Simmer for 1 minute, stir in the butter and heat for a further minute before serving.

Crab Venetian style

Preparation: 45 minutes

4 spider crabs, total weight
   2¼ lb
salt and pepper
1 bunch parsley
¼ cup oil
1 lemon

1   Plunge the crabs into boiling salted water and cook for 6 minutes.

2   Drain the crabs and leave to cool; pull away the legs and crack open with a nutcracker. Remove the flesh and chop finely.

3   Turn the crab over and pull the body away from the shell. Using a teaspoon, scrape out the eggs and set aside.

4   Remove all the meat (discard the gray stomach sac and "dead men's fingers") from the shell.

5   Finely chop the meat and add to the chopped flesh from the legs. Reserve the shells.

6   Finely chop the parsley.

7   Spoon the chopped meat back into the reserved shells and place a spoonful of the eggs in the center of each. Sprinkle with chopped parsley and season with oil, lemon juice, salt and pepper.

Crab Louis

Preparation: 1 hour

1 2¾-lb crab
salt
1 lettuce
2 tomatoes
2 hard-boiled eggs
1 small avocado
1¼ cups mayonnaise
3 tbsp chopped onion
4 tbsp chili sauce
1 tbsp Worcestershire
   sauce
Cayenne pepper
2 tbsp chopped parsley
1 tbsp lemon juice
½ cup whipped cream

1 Plunge the crab into boiling salted water and cook for 20 minutes until it turns bright red. Allow to cool slightly before extracting the meat from the body, claws, and legs (see page 125).

2 Cut the lettuce into strips, rinse and drain. Arrange on a serving dish with the crabmeat on top.

3 Cut the tomatoes, eggs, and avocado into wedges and arrange around the crabmeat.

4 In a bowl blend together the mayonnaise, onions, chili sauce, Worcestershire sauce, Cayenne pepper, chopped parsley, and lemon juice.

5 Fold in the whipped cream.

6 Spoon the sauce over the crabmeat and serve.

Potted crab

Preparation: 1 hour

1 2¾-lb crab
salt
¾ teaspoon Cayenne
    pepper
¼ teaspoon nutmeg
pinch mace
1 lemon
4 tbsp butter
2 tbsp clarified butter*

1   Plunge the crab into boiling salted water and cook for 20 minutes.

2   Break off the claws and legs. Pull off and discard the gray feathery gills ("dead men's fingers") and the gray stomach sac. Spoon out the meat and separate the white from the creamier, darker part. Crack the claws and extract the meat.

3   Place the meat in two separate bowls. Season with salt, Cayenne pepper, nutmeg, mace, and lemon juice.

4   Spoon into 4 ramekins in alternate layers of light and dark meat.

5   Melt the butter and divide equally between the ramekins.

6   Place the ramekins in a *bain-marie*; bake in a preheated oven at 325°F for 15 minutes.

7   Allow to cool before turning out.

8   Pour a little clarified butter over each one and serve with toasted bread.

Scampi in tomato and white wine sauce

Preparation: 30 minutes

20 scampi (Norway
    lobsters)
4 tbsp oil
2 cloves garlic
salt and black pepper
12 oz tomatoes
scant 1 cup white wine
1 tbsp chopped parsley

1   Rinse the scampi and with a sharp knife cut each one in half down the back.

2   Heat the oil in a large skillet.

3   Coarsely chop the garlic and fry gently in the oil for 2 minutes.

4   Remove the garlic with a slotted spoon.

5   Place the scampi side by side on their backs in the flavored oil.

6   Season with salt and plenty of freshly ground black pepper, then spoon over the coarsely chopped tomatoes. Cook for 2 minutes.

7   Pour in the white wine, cover, and simmer for 10 minutes. Sprinkle the scampi with chopped parsley and continue cooking uncovered for a further 2 minutes. Season with more black pepper and serve at once.

Chili fried scampi

15 scampi or crayfish,
  preferably raw
oil for frying
1 tsp finely chopped garlic
1 tbsp chopped leek
1 tsp finely chopped
  ginger
1 tbsp rice wine
1 tsp cornstarch

For the sauce:
½ cup chicken stock
½ cup tomato ketchup
1 tsp salt
½ tbsp sugar
1 tsp Tabasco sauce

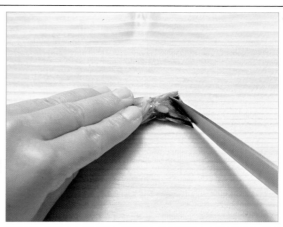

1   Rinse and drain the scampi or crayfish; remove the heads by bending them over and inward, toward the tails. Remove the shells.

2   Slit the scampi down their backs with a sharp knife, stopping short of the second to last joint nearest the tail and being careful not to cut through or the scampi will separate into two halves.

3   Remove the black vein of the scampi using a cocktail stick.

4   Rinse the scampi and dry with paper towels. Snip off the tail flippers with scissors.

5   Spread the scampi on paper towels and remove excess moisture by pressing carefully with the flat of a knife blade.

6   Heat plenty of oil in a wok or deep-fryer to 340°F and lower the scampi carefully into the hot oil; stir with chopsticks or tongs, remove, and drain. Chop the garlic, leek and ginger.

7   Heat 2 tablespoons oil in the wok and stir-fry the garlic, leek and ginger; when these start to release their aroma, add the scampi.

8   Pour in the rice wine and the sauce ingredients; stir-fry to make sure the scampi are well flavored, and then stir in the cornstarch dissolved in 2 teaspoons water to thicken the sauce so that it will coat the scampi.

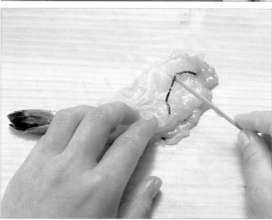

Curried jumbo shrimp

Preparation: 1 hour 10 minutes

2¼ lb jumbo shrimp
salt
½ onion
1 tomato
1 clove garlic
6 tbsp oil
¼ cup plain yogurt
½ tsp powdered ginger
½ chili pepper
1 tsp turmeric
½ tsp cumin
1 tbsp wine vinegar
½ tsp sugar
½ cup long-grain rice

1   Blanch the shrimp in boiling salted water for 3 minutes and then remove the shells.

2   Chop the onion. Blanch and peel the tomato and remove the seeds.

3   In a blender or food processor mix together all the ingredients, with the exception of the onion and shrimp, until the sauce is well blended.

4   Heat the oil in a skillet and cook the shrimp for 5 minutes. Remove with a slotted spoon and drain.

5   Fry the onion until tender in the same saucepan in the remaining oil for 5 minutes.

6   Add the sauce from the blender to the saucepan and bring to a boil.

7   Lower the heat and simmer gently for 8 minutes, stirring occasionally, until the sauce has reduced slightly.

8   Add the shrimp and cook for 3 minutes. Serve on a bed of steamed rice and garnish with chopped parsley.

Shrimp à la créole

Preparation: 40 minutes

1¾ lb cooked shrimp
2 small onions
1 celery stalk
1 small green pepper
1 clove garlic
12 oz ripe tomatoes
6 oz long-grain rice
1½ tbsp oil
4 tbsp butter
½ bay leaf
pinch thyme
1 tsp paprika
2 drops Tabasco
salt

1 Shell and rinse the shrimp.

2 Chop the onions and celery. Dice the green pepper and chop the garlic. Remove the seeds from the tomatoes and chop.

3 Steam the rice for 16 minutes.

4 Heat the oil and butter in a skillet. Add the onion, celery and pepper and fry for 5 minutes. Add the garlic and cook for 1 minute.

5 Add the bay leaf, thyme, paprika, Tabasco, and tomatoes. Season with salt.

6 Bring to a boil, lower the heat, and simmer for 15 minutes.

7 Stir in the shrimp and cook for another 4 minutes. Serve with the steamed rice.

Oysters Florentine

Preparation: 1 hour

24 fresh oysters
14 oz lightly boiled fresh
  spinach (or use frozen)
1 large shallot
¾ cup dry white wine
1¾ cups fish stock*
¼ cup butter
¼ cup flour
1 cup cream
2 egg yolks
1 tsp oil
1 tsp lemon juice
salt
white pepper

1 Scrub the shells and with an oyster knife or other very strong knife, prize the shell open and remove the oyster.

2 Pour the liquor from the shells through a fine sieve into a bowl.

3 Chop the shallot finely and sauté in half the butter until pale golden brown. Add the oysters and the dry white wine and simmer, stirring and turning gently, for 2–3 minutes. Season with a little salt and freshly ground white pepper.

Remove the oysters with a slotted spoon and keep warm.

4 Melt the remaining butter in another saucepan. Stir in the flour and gradually mix in the hot fish stock. Stir until the sauce has thickened and then add the oyster liquor, the lemon juice and a little more salt if necessary. Finally, beat the egg yolks with the cream and gradually stir into the sauce. Remove from heat.

5 Rinse the spinach very well and heat gently for 5 minutes with no added water and with a pinch of salt. Refresh under cold water, chop coarsely and warm in the wine and juices left over from cooking the oysters.

6 Place the carefully cleaned oyster shells on a lightly greased cookie sheet and fill each shell with spinach; top with an oyster. Coat with a spoonful of sauce and bake in a preheated oven at 400°F for 20 minutes.

Chilled oyster soup

Preparation: 30 minutes
(+ 2 hours for chilling)

1¾ lb oysters
¼ cup butter
2 slices bacon
1 onion
½ cup flour
scant 4½ cups milk
3 tbsp sherry
generous 1 cup light
    cream
2 tbsp chopped parsley
salt
pepper
½ tsp paprika

1   Prize open the shells over a bowl using a strong, short-bladed knife. Remove the oysters and reserve the liquid.

2   Melt the butter and gently fry the finely chopped bacon and onion for 5 minutes.

3   Sprinkle in the flour and cook for 1 minute, stirring constantly.

4   Add the very hot milk and the reserved oyster liquid. Boil for 3 minutes until thickened.

5   Remove from the heat and add the sherry and cream, stirring thoroughly until well blended.

6   Add the oysters and 1 tablespoon parsley and cook for 5 minutes over moderate heat. Season with salt and pepper.

7   Leave to cool, then refrigerate for 2 hours. Serve in individual bowls, and sprinkle with paprika and chopped parsley.

Creamed oysters

Preparation: 30 minutes

32 oysters
1¼ cups milk
1½ cups light cream
pinch celery seeds
1½ tbsp butter
salt and pepper
pinch paprika

1   Prize open the oysters with a short-bladed knife and cut them from the shell. Strain the liquor into a small bowl and reserve.

2   Heat the milk and cream in a small saucepan; add the celery seeds and 2 tablespoons of the oyster liquor and boil for 5 minutes. Strain through a fine sieve.

3   Melt the butter in a separate saucepan. Add the oysters with 2 tablespoons of the reserved liquor and cook gently for 3 minutes. Remove from the heat.

4   Add the milk and cream, season with salt and pepper, and cook for a further 2 minutes.

5   Arrange the oysters in heated bowls and cover with the creamy sauce.

6   Sprinkle with paprika and serve at once.

Scallops in white wine

Preparation: 40 minutes
(+ 1 hour for cleaning the scallops)

16 scallops
2 leeks
4 tbsp butter
salt
1 cup Riesling (or other
  medium-dry white
  wine)
pepper

1   Leave the scallops under cold running water for 1 hour. Prize the shells open and cut out the scallop, discarding the black gristly part around the cushion.

2   Cut the white part of the leeks into strips.

3   Melt the butter and fry the leeks briefly. Sprinkle with salt and pour in the wine.

4   Cook gently for 5 minutes. Add the scallops and cook, covered, for a further 5 minutes.

5   Remove the scallops and leeks and keep warm.

6   Reduce the sauce over medium heat. Place a layer of leeks on each plate; top with scallops, sprinkle with pepper, and cover with sauce.

Sea date soup

Preparation: 1 hour
(+ 2 hours for cleaning the
sea dates)

2¼ lb sea dates
8 tbsp oil
2 cloves garlic
1½ tbsp chopped parsley
pinch Cayenne pepper
1¼ cups light cream
1 tsp meat extract
1 cup canned tomatoes
1 cup white wine
salt

1   Rinse the sea dates, preferably under running water, for 2 hours, to remove all traces of sand.

2   Drain them and heat for 4 minutes in a covered skillet until they open. Remove from their shells.

3   Reserve the cooking liquor and strain through a fine sieve.

4   Pour the oil into another skillet and gently heat the finely chopped garlic.

5   Add 1 tablespoon parsley, the Cayenne pepper, cream, meat extract, tomatoes, wine, and reserved liquor.

6   Cook for 15 minutes, then strain through a fine sieve into a saucepan.

7   Add the sea dates and heat for 2 minutes. Adjust the seasoning. Sprinkle with the remaining chopped parsley and serve with slices of hot fried or toasted bread.

Mediterranean fish stew

Serves 8

Preparation: 1 hour
30 minutes

4 medium-sized onions
scant ½ cup oil
1 lb fish trimmings (tails,
  heads, bones, etc.)
5 large ripe tomatoes
1 lb shellfish (fresh,
  preferably uncooked)
2–3½ lb assorted fresh
  fish (monkfish, turbot,
  sole, mussels, hake,
  whiting, etc.)

¾ cup dry white wine
1 clove garlic
1 bouquet garni
1 packet saffron threads
salt and pepper

*For the accompanying
  sauce:*
3 egg yolks
1 clove garlic
1 cup good-quality olive
  oil
salt and pepper

To prepare the sauce:
Place the egg yolks in a
fairly large bowl and beat
together with the crushed
garlic clove; continue
stirring briskly in the same
direction, adding the oil a
few drops at a time. Season.
The sauce can be turned
an attractive orange color
by adding a little of the
saffron-colored fish stock.

1   Peel the onions, slice very thinly and heat gently in the oil in a large, heavy-bottomed saucepan.

2   Continue cooking, stirring frequently, until the onions are golden brown.

3   Add the fish trimmings and stir for a few minutes over fairly high heat; pour in the dry white wine, season with a little salt and freshly ground pepper and bring to a boil. Pour in enough water to completely cover and bring back to a boil.

4   Blanch, peel and remove the seeds from the tomatoes; chop coarsely and add to the pan. Crush the garlic and add, together with the bouquet garni; simmer for 20 minutes.

5   Strain the mixture through a fine sieve and return to a clean saucepan.

6   Soak the saffron threads in half a cup of hot water and add to the strained fish stock. Bring again to a boil.

7   Lower the larger pieces of fish into the hot stock and after about 10 minutes add the smaller fillets and the shellfish. Continue simmering until all the fish is cooked; do not stir, simply shake the saucepan from time to time to prevent the fish sticking to the bottom. Adjust the seasoning. Serve this fish stew piping hot with toasted garlic bread sprinkled with Parmesan. Pass the sauce around separately in a bowl or sauceboat.

Manhattan clam chowder

Preparation: 1 hour
20 minutes (+ 2 hours for
cleaning the clams)

2¼ lb clams
6 oz fatty bacon
1 medium onion
1 carrot
1 celery stalk
1 cup canned tomatoes
1 bay leaf
pinch thyme
salt and pepper
2 small potatoes

1   Rinse the clams,
preferably under running
water, for 2 hours, to
remove all traces of sand.

2   Place the clams in a
saucepan; cover and cook
for 3 minutes or until the
shells open. Strain and
reserve the cooking liquid.

3   Remove the clams
from their shells.

4   Chop the fatty bacon
and fry for 1 minute. Add
the chopped onion,
carrot, and celery and
cook for 5 minutes.

5   Add the tomatoes, bay
leaf, thyme, and reserved
cooking liquid from the
clams. Season with salt
and pepper and cook for 6
minutes.

6   Add 4 ladles of water
and bring to a boil. Lower
the heat, add the peeled
and diced potatoes, and
simmer for 20 minutes.

7   Add the clams and
heat gently for 2 minutes
before serving.

Moules marinière

Preparation: 20 minutes
(+ 2 hours for cleaning the mussels)

4½ lb mussels
1 onion
3 shallots
1 clove garlic
3 tbsp butter
1⅛ cups white wine
½ bay leaf
pinch thyme
black pepper
3 tbsp chopped parsley

1   Scrub the mussels thoroughly, removing the beard-like threads, and leave under running water for 2 hours to rinse free of sand.

2   Chop the onion, shallots, and garlic.

3   Melt the butter in a large saucepan and gently fry the onion and shallots until tender. Add the garlic and cook for a further 1 minute.

4   Add the wine, bay leaf, thyme, and black pepper and cook for 2 minutes.

5   Add the mussels and cook for 5 minutes, shaking the saucepan occasionally, until all the shells have opened. Discard any which have not.

6   Sprinkle with parsley and serve the mussels in bowls with the cooking liquid.

Cuttlefish with peas

Preparation: 40 minutes

1¾ lb cuttlefish (or squid)
½ onion
½ cup white wine
salt and pepper
8 oz tomatoes
14 oz shelled peas
½ tsp sugar
1 sprig rosemary

1   Remove the central bone of the cuttlefish by pressing in the end of the sac-like body and pulling from the opposite end. The head will pull away, together with the bone, the ink sac, and entrails. Reserve the tentacles and discard the rest. Rinse and dry the cuttlefish, rubbing off the purplish skin; cut in half lengthwise and chop into strips 2 inches long.

2   Finely chop the onion and brown in the oil.

3   After 4 minutes add the strips of cuttlefish and chopped tentacles.

4   Cook for 5 minutes, then pour in the wine. Season with salt, cover, and cook for a further 5 minutes.

5   Add the skinned, seeded, and chopped tomatoes and cook, uncovered, over high heat for 5 minutes.

6   Add the peas and sugar.

7   Cook for a further 15 minutes. Add the rosemary, adjust the seasoning and sprinkle with pepper. Reduce the sauce by boiling vigorously for 1 minute, then serve.

Stuffed squid

Preparation: 1 hour

8 squid, total weight 1¾ lb
8 black olives, pitted
1 tbsp capers
2 tbsp chopped parsley
2 drops Tabasco
2 drops Worcestershire
  sauce
1 tbsp breadcrumbs
½ cup oil
1 clove garlic
2 tomatoes
salt and black pepper
pinch oregano

1   Cut off the tentacles, remove and discard the ink sac attached to the head. Pull out and discard the central transparent "pen" and rub off the purplish outer skin.

2   Chop the tentacles.

3   Finely chop the olives, capers, and parsley.

4   Place all the chopped ingredients, including the tentacles, in a bowl and add 2 drops each of Tabasco and Worcestershire sauce, the breadcrumbs, and 2 tablespoons oil. Mix well.

5   Stuff each squid with a little filling and carefully sew the ends with kitchen thread.

6   Finely chop the garlic and the skinned and seeded tomatoes.

7   Pour the remaining oil into a large skillet. Gently fry the chopped garlic over very low heat for 2 minutes. Add the chopped tomatoes and cook for a further 2 minutes.

8   Add the stuffed squid and a little salt. Cover and simmer for 20 minutes. Sprinkle with oregano and black pepper and cook for 3 minutes. Serve immediately.

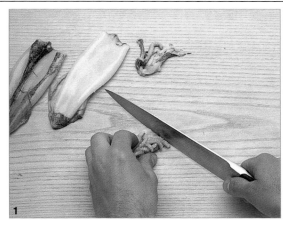

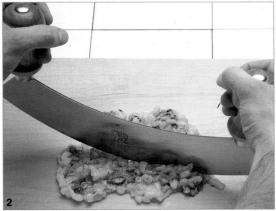

Coulibiac of salmon

Preparation: 1 hour
30 minutes

8 oz fresh salmon
½ cup butter
salt and pepper
½ tsp paprika
½ tsp dried dill
¼ cup white wine
½ lemon
3 shallots
¾ cup rice
2 cups chicken stock
3 eggs (2 hard-boiled)
1 tbsp chopped parsley
6 oz mushrooms
2 tbsp chopped chives
14 oz puff pastry
sour cream (optional)

1   Cut the salmon into chunks and place in a buttered baking pan. Sprinkle with salt, paprika, and dill. Pour the wine and lemon juice over the salmon. Cover with foil and place in a preheated oven (350°F) for 15 minutes.

2   Melt a quarter of the butter in a small saucepan and brown 2 chopped shallots for 1 minute. Add the rice, stir for 1 minute, then pour in the stock and cook for 15 minutes.

3   Stir into the rice two chopped hard-boiled eggs, the parsley, and salt and pepper.

4   Melt 2 tablespoons butter in another pan; add the remaining finely chopped shallot and the sliced mushrooms and cook for 6 minutes. Sprinkle with salt and the chopped chives.

5   Roll out the pastry into a rectangle ¼ inch thick. Arrange alternate layers of rice, salmon, and mushrooms in the center, leaving a generous amount of pastry to fold over.

6   Brush down one side of the pastry with beaten egg. Fold over the other side to enclose the filling and press down gently to seal the edge.

7   Place the salmon roll on a buttered baking sheet. Cut decorative leaves with any remaining pastry. Leave two holes for the steam to escape, then brush the roll with beaten egg. Leave to stand for 20 to 30 minutes. Bake at 400°F for 10 minutes, then lower to 375°F for 30 minutes.

8   Leave to cool for 15 minutes, then pour melted butter into the holes. Serve with more melted butter or sour cream.

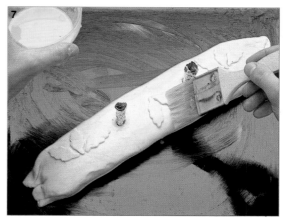

Gravlax

Preparation: 1 hour
(+ 1 day for the salmon to
stand)

bunch dill
5 peppercorns
1 1¾-lb fresh salmon
4½ tbsp sugar
1 tbsp sea salt
2 tbsp Dijon mustard
2 tbsp white wine vinegar
½ cup oil
1 lemon

1   Rinse and dry the dill
and crush the
peppercorns.

2   Remove the head and
cut the salmon in half.
Remove the backbone
using a sharp knife and
leave the skin intact. Rinse
and dry well.

3   In a small bowl mix
together 3 tablespoons
sugar, the salt, and the
crushed peppercorns.

4   Place half the salmon,
skin side down, in a long
shallow dish and sprinkle
with 1 tablespoon
chopped dill and the
mixture of salt, sugar, and
pepper. Place the other
half, skin side up, on top.

5   Wrap in foil, cover
with another plate and
place a 6½-pound weight
on top. Refrigerate for at
least 24 hours. Turn after
12 hours, spooning over
the juices.

6   Place the salmon on a
chopping board and slice
off thin pieces diagonally.

7   Prepare the sauce: mix
together the mustard,
remaining sugar, and
vinegar. Blend in the oil
gradually. Add the
remaining chopped dill.

8   Arrange the slices on a
serving dish, cover with
the sauce, and garnish
with lemon wedges. Serve
any remaining sauce
separately.

Anguilles au vert

Preparation: 1 hour

4 oz fresh sorrel
2 tbsp chopped parsley
6 leaves tarragon
3 leaves sage
2 eels, total weight 2¼ lb
4 tbsp butter
salt and pepper
1¼ cups white wine
2 egg yolks
1½ tbsp lemon juice

1   Rinse and finely chop the sorrel. Chop the parsley, tarragon, and sage.

2   Rinse and skin the eels. Divide in half lengthwise, remove the backbone, and cut into 2½-inch pieces.

3   Brown the pieces of eel in the butter for 5 minutes. Add the sorrel and other chopped herbs. Season with salt and pepper and pour in the wine.

4   Bring to a boil, lower the heat, and simmer for 15 minutes. Transfer the eel pieces to a serving dish.

5   Beat the egg yolks with a little of the cooking liquid, then pour into the saucepan.

6   Heat gently for 3 minutes, stirring constantly, until the sauce thickens. Add the lemon juice.

7   Pour the sauce over the eel and leave to cool before serving.

Eel pie

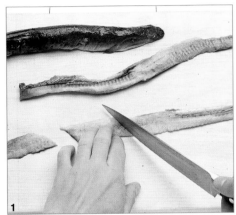

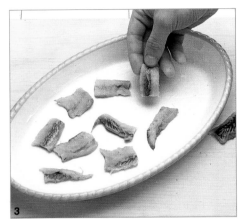

Preparation: 1 hour
20 minutes

1 2¼-lb eel
6 tbsp butter
1 large shallot
scant 1 cup Marsala
pinch nutmeg
1 tbsp chopped parsley
salt and pepper
½ cup flour
juice of ½ lemon
2 hard-boiled eggs
2 oz frozen shortcrust
    pastry

1   Rinse and skin the eel (see page 155), and cut into 2-inch pieces.

2   Melt 2 tablespoons butter in a skillet and brown the finely chopped shallot. Add the Marsala, nutmeg, parsley, scant 1 cup water, salt and pepper, and cook for 4 minutes.

3   Place the pieces of eel in a large buttered ovenproof pan.

4   Melt the remaining butter and stir in the flour. Cook gently for 1 minute.

5   Stir in the mixture from the skillet and the lemon juice. Bring to a boil, stirring constantly, and cook for 3 minutes.

6   Pour the sauce over the eel. Place the slices of hard-boiled egg on top and cover with the rolled-out pastry. Bake in a preheated oven at 450°F for 10 minutes, then lower to 350°F for 30 minutes.

Carp Jewish style

Preparation: 1 hour
15 minutes (+ 2 hours for
chilling)

1 2¾-lb carp
½ cup blanched almonds
1 onion
2 shallots
12 tbsp oil
2 tbsp flour
1 tbsp sugar
1¼ cups fish stock*
⅓ cup seedless white
  raisins
1 bouquet garni
1 clove garlic
salt and pepper
1 tbsp chopped parsley

1   Clean and rinse the carp.

2   Chop the almonds into thin slivers.

3   Finely chop the onion and shallots.

4   Pour half the oil into a skillet. Add the chopped onion and shallots and fry for 2 minutes.

5   Stir in the flour and sugar and cook for 2 minutes before adding the fish stock, almonds, and seedless white raisins.

6   Place the carp in a fish kettle with the bouquet garni and crushed garlic. Pour over the sauce.

7   Heat gently for a few minutes before seasoning with salt and pepper. Cook over moderate heat for a further 30 minutes.

8   Drain the carp and place on a serving dish. Reduce the cooking liquid by boiling vigorously. Discard the bouquet garni and add the remaining oil, stirring with a balloon whisk. Adjust the seasoning and allow to cool before pouring the sauce over the fish. Chill for at least 2 hours and sprinkle with chopped parsley before serving.

Stuffed pike

Preparation: 1 hour
15 minutes (+ 45 minutes
for soaking the prunes)

15 prunes
1 2¼-lb pike
½ cup long-grain rice
salt and pepper
3 hard-boiled eggs
4 tbsp butter
dry breadcrumbs

1 Soak the prunes in warm water for 45 minutes. Drain them, pit; chop half of them coarsely. Reserve the remaining prunes.

2 Remove the scales, clean, rinse, and dry the pike. Sprinkle with salt.

3 Cook the rice in boiling salted water for 12 to 15 minutes or until tender. Chop the hard-boiled eggs.

4 Stuff the pike with a mixture of rice, egg, the chopped prunes, salt and pepper, and half the butter.

5 Sew up the cavity of the fish with kitchen thread.

6 Coat the fish in the breadcrumbs.

7 Place in a buttered roasting pan and dot with the remaining butter.

8 Bake in a preheated oven at 300°F for 15 minutes, then raise the heat to 400°F for a further 10 minutes or until cooked. Remove the thread. Serve on a bed of rice and garnish with the remaining prunes.

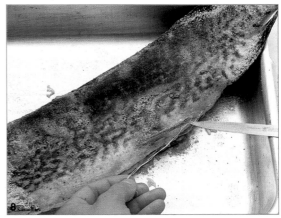

Stuffed trout with almonds

Preparation: 1 hour
15 minutes

4 boned whole trout
2 eggs
1 cup soft breadcrumbs
milk
2 onions
2 scallions or shallots
1 cup dry white wine
1 tbsp butter
few tbsps fine
    breadcrumbs
½ cup slivered almonds
½ cup oil
salt and pepper

1   Hard-boil an egg, place under cold running water, shell, and mash with a fork. Moisten the soft breadcrumbs with a little milk, squeeze well and then mix with the mashed hard-boiled egg.

2   Sauté the finely chopped onion and scallions or shallots gently in 3 tablespoons oil, season with salt and pepper and then blend with the breadcrumb and egg mixture. Stir in the remaining egg.

3   Fill the cavity of each trout with a quarter of this stuffing.

4   Sew up the sides of the trout or secure with cocktail sticks.

5   Brush the trout with oil and coat with fine breadcrumbs.

6   Arrange the trout in a lightly greased ovenproof dish and pour in the white wine.

7   Sprinkle the slivered almonds over the fish.

8   Grease a piece of foil and place on top of the trout, buttered side down. Bake in a preheated oven (350°F) for about 30 minutes, spooning some of the wine and cooking juices over the fish occasionally to keep moist. Remove the foil after twenty minutes to allow almonds to brown. Serve immediately.

Meat, Poultry, and Game

Veal and mushrooms Istanbul

Preparation: 1 hour

1¾ lb veal escalopes,
    thinly sliced from the leg
⅓ cup oil
juice of ½ lemon
1 large onion
¾ cup dry white wine
½ pint light stock
3 cups mushrooms
1 tbsp tomato paste
1 oz bacon
scant ½ cup cream
paprika
salt and pepper
cornstarch (optional)

1   Clean the mushrooms and place in a bowl of water mixed with the lemon juice to prevent them from discoloring. Dry and slice just before sautéing.

2   Chop the onion and the bacon; sauté in a saucepan in 2 tablespoons oil. As soon as the onion starts to turn brown, add the sliced mushrooms. Stir and fry gently over moderate heat for about 10 minutes. Season with a pinch of salt and a little freshly ground pepper. Remove from heat.

3   Pound the veal slices with a meat mallet dipped in cold water; trim off any fat and cut into strips.

4   Dust the strips of veal with flour, place in a sieve and shake to get rid of excess flour.

5   Sauté the strips in the remaining oil over fairly high heat; turn so that they color evenly and sprinkle with a pinch of salt. Using a slotted spoon, transfer the veal strips to a heated dish, cover and keep warm.

6   Stir the wine into the juices in the pan, stirring with a wooden spoon until the wine has almost completely evaporated.

7   Stir in the tomato paste and the light stock (preferably veal stock); then dribble in the cream while stirring.

8   Add the sautéed vegetables and bacon to the sauce, then the veal strips. Stir until every strip of veal is coated with sauce and sprinkle with a generous pinch of paprika. Cook for 10–15 minutes until the sauce has reduced slightly. Thicken with a little cornstarch dissolved in cold water if desired. Serve with pilaf rice*.

167

Classic veal fricassée

Preparation: 2 hours

2¼ lb veal, cut into small
   cubes
3½ pints light stock
1 small carrot, 1 leek and
   1 onion stuck with a
   clove
1 bouquet garni
¼ lb skinned baby onions
6 oz mushrooms

generous ¼ cup butter
½ cup flour
3 egg yolks
generous ½ cup cream
juice of ¼ lemon
grated nutmeg
1 tbsp finely chopped
   parsley
salt and pepper

1 Place the cubed veal in a large saucepan and pour in enough strained stock to cover by at least ¾ in. Bring to a gentle boil and continue cooking while skimming off the scum from the top.

2 Add the carrot, leek, onion and bouquet garni and continue to simmer gently for 1 hour 50 minutes.

3 Cook the onions separately for about 40 minutes, adding 2 tablespoons butter, 3 tablespoons water and a pinch of salt so that they are lightly glazed when done.

4 Clean, trim and thinly slice the mushrooms and boil for about 10 minutes in a generous ½ cup water.

5 Strain the veal and reserve the cooking stock; place the veal in another saucepan and add the onions and strained mushrooms; keep warm.

6 Melt the remaining butter, stir in the flour and then gradually stir in the hot stock from the veal.

7 Cook the sauce over low heat for 15 minutes, stirring with a wooden spoon and removing any scum that collects during cooking. Beat the egg yolks with the cream and a few drops of lemon juice; dribble this into the veal stock sauce, stirring continuously and briskly so that the egg mixture will not curdle. Add a pinch of nutmeg and bring almost to a boil.

8 Pour the sauce through a sieve onto the veal, onions and mushrooms and stir the veal in the sauce over a low heat; remove from heat as soon as it starts to boil and transfer to a deep, warm serving dish. Sprinkle with parsley and serve.

Roast tenderloin of beef with wine sauce

Preparation: 1 hour
10 minutes

2¼ lb beef tenderloin
1½ pints beef stock
½ lb cubed lean beef
1 onion
1 carrot
1 celery stalk
1 tsp tomato paste
¾ cup dry white wine
scant ½ cup cornstarch
⅔ cup oil
salt and pepper
watercress

1   If not already done, tie the meat with string so that it will hold its shape while cooking.

2   Sprinkle generously with salt and freshly ground pepper.

3   Heat 6 tablespoons oil in a heavy sauté pan or skillet over fairly high heat and add the beef; cook for 15 minutes to seal the flavor and brown evenly all over. Remove the meat from the oil.

4   Wrap the beef in foil and then wrap in a towel. Keep warm (this way the meat will not dry out or toughen).

5   Trim, wash and prepare the vegetables. Chop the onion coarsely, dice the carrot and celery; sauté in the remaining 6 tablespoons of oil.

6   Transfer the vegetables to a second sauté pan or heavy-bottomed casserole, add the cubed beef; stir and sauté for a few minutes before seasoning with salt and pepper. Add the wine and when this has almost completely evaporated, sprinkle in the cornstarch.

7   Stir in the tomato paste mixed with the hot stock; simmer over moderate heat for 40 minutes, skimming off any scum from the surface.

8   Strain off the cooking liquid into a saucepan; blend the diced beef and the vegetables in a food processor. Pour this mixture back into the cooking liquid and bring to a boil. Remove the wrappings and string from the tenderloin, cut into fairly thick slices and garnish with watercress. Serve the sauce very hot, passing it around separately.

Beef olives

Preparation: 1 hour
50 minutes

8 fairly thin pieces of beef
(such as flank steak, cut
against the grain, or
rump roast cut into
cross-grained slices),
each trimmed to
measure about 8 in × 8
in
1 large onion
2 carrots

1 celery stalk
4 large ripe tomatoes
1 pint tomato juice
scant 1 cup red wine
3 tbsp oil
3 tbsp butter
1 oz *beurre manié*
3 tbsp milk
salt and pepper

For the stuffing:
1 cup lean ground pork
1 cup finely chopped or
ground lean beef
pinch thyme
pinch powdered bay leaf
few ground fennel seeds
pinch ground coriander
salt and pepper

1   Cover the slices of beef with plastic wrap and beat gently with a meat mallet.

2   Prepare the filling: place the ground pork and beef in a bowl and add the seasonings and herbs; mix well until all the ingredients have combined in a smooth paste.

3   Place two flattened pieces of beef so that they slightly overlap, place a quarter of the stuffing in the middle and roll up, tying firmly with string.

4   Heat 2 tablespoons butter in a skillet with the oil. When it is very hot add the beef olives and brown on all sides. Season with salt and pepper, remove from skillet and keep warm.

5   Clean and trim the carrots and celery and peel the onion before chopping into small pieces. Melt the remaining butter in a large saucepan, add the vegetables and sweat gently over low heat.

6   Add the beef olives, pour in the wine and, as soon as it has evaporated, add the peeled, seeded and diced tomatoes and the tomato juice; stir and then leave to simmer gently for about 30 minutes. Remove the beef olives from the saucepan and keep hot on a heated serving platter.

7   Add the milk to the sauce and beat in with a whisk or hand-held beater.

8   Add the *beurre manié*. Season with a little salt and freshly ground pepper. Push the sauce through a sieve (or blend in an electric blender or food processor) and pour over the beef olives, some of which can be sliced and ready to serve.

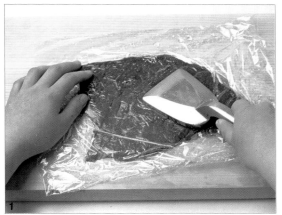

Argentine braised beef

Serves 6

Preparation: 2 hours
50 minutes

3 lb rump roast, cut into
   1-in cubes
generous ¼ cup
   shortening
⅓ cup oil
2 large onions
2 green peppers
5 large ripe tomatoes
1 celery stalk
3 medium potatoes
10 oz pumpkin (skin and
   seeds removed)

2 small apples
2 cups cooked sweet corn
   (fresh or canned)
5 oz grapes
1 bouquet garni
1¼ cups dry white wine
1½ cups stock
generous 1 cup rice
3 peppercorns
1 clove garlic
salt
cayenne pepper

This dish is spectacular
when served in a
pumpkin. Prepare the
pumpkin by slicing off the
top, scooping out all the
seeds and washing the
inside; heat for 15 minutes
in a hot oven.
Alternatively, serve the
beef in a rustic-looking
deep earthenware dish.

1   Brown the beef in the melted, very hot shortening in a large, heavy-bottomed casserole or enamel pot.

2   Sauté the sliced onions, the crushed clove of garlic and the peppers (seeds and pith removed and coarsely chopped) in the oil over gentle heat, using an earthenware or cast iron pot or skillet. Add the chopped tomatoes.

3   When the vegetables have cooked through, transfer them with their juices to the casserole containing the meat. While stirring, add the chopped celery and the bouquet garni. Season with salt, cayenne pepper and the peppercorns.

4   Add the white wine a little at a time. When this is considerably reduced, pour in the hot stock and stir. Cover and cook over low heat for 1 hour 15 minutes, stirring at frequent intervals.

5   While the beef and vegetables are simmering, peel and dice the potatoes, apples and pumpkin. Stir into the meat and vegetable mixture when it has cooked for the length of time given above. Continue cooking for a further 30 minutes.

6   Stir in the cooked, drained sweet corn.

7   While the beef is braising cook the rice in plenty of salted boiling water; when it is tender but not mushy drain and then stir into the beef together with the grapes. Adjust the seasoning and cook for a few minutes longer. Serve immediately in a large, heated earthenware dish or, for a better effect, in a large pumpkin.

Marinated roast beef

Preparation: 2 hours
50 minutes (+ 2 days for
marinating the beef)

2¼ lb rib eye or rump
   roast
⅓ cup oil
few tbsp all-purpose flour
1 medium onion
1 carrot
1 celery stalk
1 clove garlic
pinch freshly grated fresh
   ginger
1 small carton yogurt
salt and pepper

For the marinade:
1 onion
2 shallots
1 carrot
2 cups dry red wine
6 tbsp red wine vinegar
1 cup water
1 bay leaf
few cumin seeds
thyme
salt
5 peppercorns

To prepare the marinade:
Wash, peel and finely slice
the onion, shallots and
carrot and place in a large
pot with the other
ingredients. Bring to a
gentle boil, stirring from
time to time; lower the
heat and simmer gently for
10 minutes. Cool to room
temperature.

1   Prepare the marinade following the instructions opposite. Immerse beef in the cooled marinade. Cover and leave in the refrigerator for two days, turning the beef several times.

2   After two days, take the beef out of the marinade and dry with paper towels. Set marinade aside. Season a few tablespoons of flour with salt and freshly ground pepper and flour the meat. Heat the oil in a large, heavy-bottomed fireproof casserole or enamel pot and brown the beef all over; when well colored, remove from pot and set aside.

3   In the same pot, sauté the finely sliced onion, carrot, celery and chopped garlic very gently for 5 minutes, stirring frequently.

4   Return the beef to the pot, pour the reserved marinade over it, add the grated fresh ginger and bring slowly to a boil.

5   As soon as the marinade starts to boil, turn down the heat, cover and simmer very slowly for 2½ hours; use two wooden spatulas or tongs to turn the beef frequently so that it cooks evenly; whisk a tablespoon of yogurt into the cooking liquid whenever the meat is turned.

6   When the beef is done, take out and allow to cool to room temperature. Strain the cooking liquid through a fine sieve, return to the pot and reheat.

7   Slice the cooled meat, place in the strained sauce and allow to heat over very low heat. Arrange the slices on a heated serving platter, cover with a little of the sauce and pass around the rest of the sauce separately.

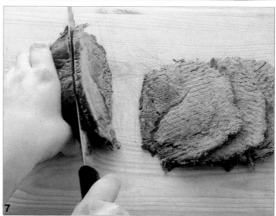

Carpetbag steaks

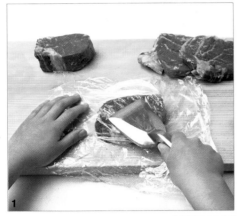
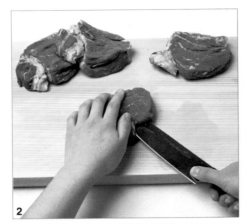
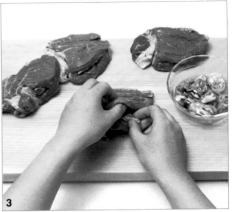

Preparation: 1 hour

4 thick club, sirloin or
   porterhouse steaks
2 tbsp butter
16 fresh oysters
salt and pepper

For the sauce:
2 finely chopped shallots
4 ripe tomatoes
1 pint stock made with a
   stock cube
½ cup port
3 tbsp butter
1 oz *beurre manié* (3 tbsp
   flour worked into 1 tbsp
   softened butter)
salt and pepper

1   Cover the steaks with
plastic wrap and pound
with a meat mallet.

2   Make an incision in
one side of each steak.

3   Push two oysters into
each steak and secure with
a cocktail stick.

4   To prepare the sauce:
Melt the butter in a
saucepan, add the shallots
and sauté until golden
brown.

5   Pour in the port and
cook until it has almost
completely evaporated.

6   Add the peeled,
seeded and roughly
chopped tomatoes, the
remaining oysters, also
chopped, and the stock;
season. Let the sauce
simmer and reduce before
adding the *beurre manié*,
stirring the mixture as the
butter melts and releases
the flour into the sauce to
thicken it. While the sauce
is reducing fry the steaks in
the very hot butter,
seasoning them. Make
sure the steaks and their
contents are warmed
through without
overcooking. Transfer the
steaks to a hot serving dish

and pour the sauce over
each one.

New England boiled beef and chicken

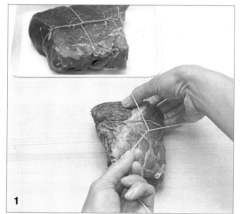

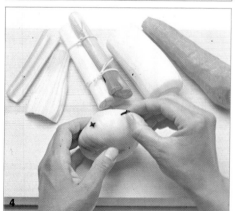

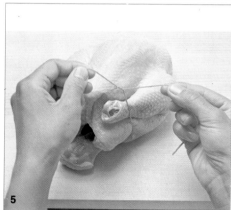

Serves 8

Preparation: 2 hours 30 minutes

2¼ lb top round steak
1¾ lb rump roast
1 2¼ lb chicken
1 small cabbage
1 onion
1 leek
2 carrots
2 celery stalks
1 clove garlic
1 turnip
2 cloves
salt

1   Tie the two cuts of beef together firmly with string.

2   Place the meat in a large pot with 3 quarts plus 1 pint water and a generous pinch of coarse salt; bring to a boil. Use a ladle to skim off the scum on the surface. Lower the heat and simmer over very low heat for at least 1 hour.

3   Wash the cabbage; remove the hard stalk and strip off the leaves. Place the leaves in groups of four, one on top of the other; roll up each pile and tie with string.

4   Wash the leek, cut in half lengthwise and tie at top and bottom. Peel the turnip and the onion; stud the onion with the two cloves. Scrape the carrots, wash the celery stalks and cut into 3–4 in lengths.

5   Wash and dry the chicken and truss with string.

6   Add the vegetables and chicken to the pot containing the beef, cover with foil or a tight-fitting lid and bring to a boil. Lower heat and simmer for 1 hour 15 minutes. Remove strings from chicken and vegetables. Serve each person with a selection of carved meats and some of the vegetables.

Jamaican loin of pork

Preparation: 1 hour
30 minutes

2¼ lb boneless loin of
   pork
½ cup oil
2 onions
2 cloves garlic
4 large ripe tomatoes
1 bouquet garni
1 cinnamon stick
¾ cup dry white wine
generous pinch grated
   nutmeg
few drops Tabasco sauce
salt and pepper

The original Jamaican
recipe calls for a garnish of
sliced bananas sautéed in
butter and seasoned with
salt and pepper, which
adds a further dimension
to the flavor and gives the
dish a more authentic,
exotic touch.

1 Tie the boned loin of pork securely so that it will keep its shape as it cooks; sprinkle with a little salt and freshly ground pepper; brown well on each side in the oil in a large, heavy-bottomed casserole or enamel pot.

2 When the pork is golden brown all over, transfer to a stainless steel plate, cover and place over a saucepan of boiling water to keep the meat warm.

3 Sauté the finely chopped onions in the oil used to brown the meat; fry very gently until transparent but do not brown; place the loin of pork on top of the onions, sprinkle with the finely chopped garlic. Blanch and peel the tomatoes, cut in quarters and remove the seeds; add to the pork. Sprinkle the grated nutmeg into the casserole and crumble in the cinnamon stick; add the bouquet garni and 2 or 3 drops of Tabasco sauce.

4 Season with a little more salt and freshly ground pepper, pour in the dry white wine, cover and bring to a gentle boil over fairly low heat. Place in a preheated oven at 400°F for 1 hour, basting frequently.

5 Remove the pork from the casserole, leaving it at room temperature to cool. Pour the cooking liquid through a fine sieve.

6 When the pork has cooled, remove the string and carve into slices. Pour a little of the strained juices into a shallow serving dish, arrange the pork slices in the dish, slightly overlapping one another, and cover with the remaining strained juices. Cover with foil and return to the oven for 10–15 minutes at 350°F.

Pork chops with figs

Preparation: 1 hour

12 small pork chops
6 tbsp oil
¾ cup dry white wine
2 gherkins
2 finely chopped shallots
6 tbsp gravy (made with
   half a stock cube
   dissolved with 1 tbsp
   butter into 1 tbsp white
   wine)
4 canned figs (drained,
   syrup reserved)

juice of ½ lemon
½ tbsp tarragon
1 tsp of syrup from the
   canned figs
½ cup cream
1 tbsp chopped parsley
1 tbsp all-purpose flour
generous ¼ cup butter
salt and pepper

The contrast between the
sharp taste of the gherkins
and the bland cream
complements the
sweetness of the figs and
gives this dish a very
unusual sweet-and-sour
flavor.

1   Season the pork chops with a little salt and freshly ground pepper.

2   Heat the oil in a large skillet and fry the pork on both sides; pour in the dry white wine and continue cooking until the wine has completely evaporated; remove the pork chops from the skillet and keep warm.

3   Melt the butter in the skillet, stir in the flour with a wooden spoon, making sure there are no lumps.

4   Add the cream, the stock, butter and wine mixture and the finely chopped gherkins and shallots.

5   Continue stirring and add the figs and the teaspoon of syrup.

6   Sprinkle the chopped tarragon and the lemon juice into the sauce and simmer for a few minutes over moderate heat to allow the sauce to reduce and thicken. Arrange the pork chops on a heated serving plate or directly onto the dinner plates, cover with sauce and sprinkle with the finely chopped parsley.

Pork chops in lemon sauce

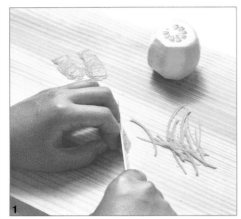

Preparation: 1 hour
20 minutes

8 pork chops
¼ cup butter
salt and pepper

For the sauce:
2 lemons
1 pint stock
¾ cup dry white wine
1 tbsp tomato paste
beurre manié (made with 1
   tbsp butter and 1 tsp
   flour)
scant 2 tbsp butter
salt and pepper

1   Remove the peel of the
lemons and cut into
julienne strips; reserve the
peeled lemons.

2   Place the julienne
strips in a saucepan, cover
with cold water, blanch for
2 minutes, then drain.

3   Heat the butter in a
skillet and fry the pork
chops until they color on
both sides; season. When
the pork is cooked
through, take up and keep
warm.

4   To prepare the sauce:
Add the wine and the
stock to the cooking juices
and heat until it has
considerably reduced.

5   Stir in the tomato
paste, remove from heat
and mix in the *beurre
manié*; return to the heat
and stir constantly.

6   Add the strips of
lemon peel and the whole
lemon segments (pith and
membrane removed).
Season. Simmer gently for
15 minutes. Pour the
sauce over the pork chops
on the serving dish or
individual plates. Serve
with creamed potatoes,
puréed carrots and a
purée of peas (piped
decoratively using a fluted
nozzle and a piping bag);
garnish with sprigs of
watercress.

Thrice-cooked pork

Preparation: 4 hours

2 lb pork belly in one
    piece
1 leek
1 piece root ginger, finely
    chopped
oil for frying
1 star anise
½ tbsp cornstarch

For the sauce:
4–6 tbsp soy sauce
1 tbsp sugar
1 tbsp rice wine
½ cup of the liquid in
    which the pork has
    been cooked

1   Bring plenty of water to a boil in a large saucepan; place the pork belly in the boiling water for a few minutes; remove and place in a fresh saucepan of boiling water together with a whole leek and the ginger. Cover and cook for approximately 35 minutes.

2   Mix the sauce ingredients.

3   When the pork is done, cool slightly, drain, and dry with paper towels. Heat plenty of oil to 350°F and fry the pork until it is well colored all over.

4   Remove the pork and immediately rinse in very cold water; when cold enough to handle, slice into pieces about ¼ inch thick.

5   Place fat side down, in a heatproof dish; add the star anise and the sauce, sprinkling it evenly over the meat.

6   Place the dish in a bamboo steamer, over boiling water producing plenty of steam; cook over moderate heat for about 2 hours, topping up the boiling water with hot water whenever needed to avoid burning the steamer.

7   Remove the dish from the steamer and cool; place in the refrigerator and remove the layer of fat which will form on the surface. Return the dish to the steamer and cook for a further 1 to 2 hours or until the pork is very tender. Transfer to a hot serving dish.

8   Pour the juices which have been produced during cooking into a saucepan, bring to a boil, and then stir in the cornstarch dissolved in 1 tablespoon cold water. Cook briefly and then pour over the pork.

1

2

3

4

5

6

7

8

Sweet and sour pork

Preparation: 30 minutes

¾ lb leg of pork (boned)
1 red chili pepper
2 leeks
1 tsp finely chopped garlic
½ small can pineapple
4 green peppers
2 tsp cornstarch
1 egg
cornstarch as required
oil for frying
1 tbsp rice wine

For the sauce:
scant ⅓ cup vinegar
1 tbsp soy sauce
4½ tbsp sugar
1 tbsp tomato ketchup
2 tbsp Worcestershire
   sauce
½ tsp salt

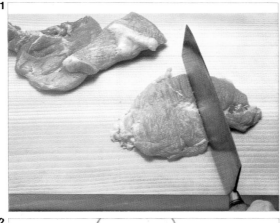

1 Cut the pork into slices about ½ inch thick and pound each piece lightly on both sides with the blunt edge of the cleaver to tenderize; then cut into bite-size portions.

2 Remove the seeds from the chili pepper and cut it into rings about ¼ inch thick. Slice the leeks into ½-inch lengths, and chop the garlic very finely.

3 Drain the pineapple and chop; slice the green peppers and cut into portions the same size as the pork.

4 Mix the sauce ingredients together. In a separate small bowl or cup dissolve 2 teaspoons cornstarch in 4 teaspoons cold water.

5 Dip the pork in the beaten egg and then coat with cornstarch. Heat the oil over medium heat in a wok and fry the pork until it is cooked through. Set aside.

6 Heat 2 tablespoons oil in the wok and stir-fry the garlic; as soon as this releases its aroma, add the leeks followed by the peppers.

7 When the peppers are tender, add the chili pepper, the pineapple, and the pork and stir-fry, mixing and turning all the ingredients briskly: moisten with the rice wine to add flavor.

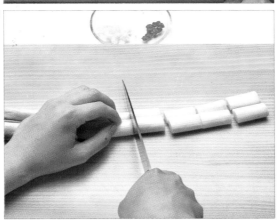

8 Finally, add the sweet and sour sauce, followed by the cornstarch dissolved in water; mix thoroughly and serve.

Pork chops with Dijon mustard sauce

Preparation: 1 hour

12 pork chops
6 tbsp oil
¾ cup dry white wine
¾ pint cream
2 onions
2 tbsp butter
6 tbsp gravy made with
    half a stock cube
    dissolved with 1 tbsp
    butter into 1½ tbsp dry
    white wine
5–6 tbsp Dijon mustard
salt and pepper

1   Trim off the fat from the pork chops with a very sharp knife.

2   Melt the butter in a skillet, add the chopped onions and sauté until a pale golden brown.

3   Heat the oil in another skillet and when very hot add the lightly floured pork chops. Brown on both sides and then season with a little salt and freshly ground pepper. Pour in the cream and finish cooking the pork chops over gentle heat; when they are done, remove them from the sauce and keep warm on a heated serving plate.

4   Stir the sautéed onions into the sauce.

5   Stir in the mustard.

6   Add the stock, butter and wine mixture and reduce over a moderate heat; pour the sauce over the pork, sprinkle with chopped parsley and serve.

192

Roast pork with prune filling

Preparation: 1 hour
40 minutes

1¾ lb boneless shoulder
  of pork
4 spareribs of pork
1 carrot
1 onion
1 stock cube
½ cup oil
¾ cup red wine
1 tbsp pearl barley
1 tbsp melted butter
1 tsp soy sauce
1 tbsp all-purpose flour
salt and pepper

For the filling:
20 dried prunes, soaked
  for 30 minutes in warm
  water, drained and then
  left to stand for 1 hour in
  red wine.

1   Unroll the shoulder roast and trim to form a triangle.

2   Drain the prunes and reserve the wine. Pit the prunes and arrange 10 of them at one end of the rectangle of pork. Sprinkle with a little salt and freshly ground pepper and roll up the meat so that the prunes end up in the middle. Tie the roll with string.

3   Pour 6 tablespoons of oil into a roasting pan, place the meat in the pan and sprinkle with salt and freshly ground pepper; arrange the spareribs, the coarsely chopped onion and carrot around the rolled pork and brush the meat with the remaining oil. Place in a preheated oven (400°F) and roast for 35 minutes, turning the pork frequently and basting with the juices.

4   When the pork is crisp and well browned, take up and set aside. Place the roasting pan over low heat and pour in the reserved heated wine into which the stock cube has been crumbled. Stir well.

5   Mix barley, 1 tablespoon melted butter, 1 teaspoon soy sauce and 1 tablespoon flour. Add this mixture to the sauce and stir until it thickens.

6   Strain the sauce through a metal sieve into a saucepan.

7   Add the remaining soaked prunes to the sauce, cook for 20 minutes over gentle heat. When the meat has cooled, remove the string and slice. Arrange in a shallow, ovenproof dish, together with some of the sauce, cover with foil and heat in the oven. Serve with the prunes and garnish with watercress. Serve the remaining sauce in a sauceboat.

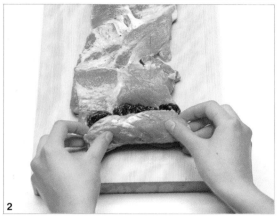

Pork crown roast

Serves 6

Preparation: 2 hours
30 minutes

9 pork spareribs, uncut

For the stuffing:
½ cup finely chopped or
   minced cooked ham
scant ½ cup finely
   chopped or minced
   pork
1 cup fresh soft
   breadcrumbs soaked in
   ½ cup milk and
   squeezed out

3 tbsp freshly grated
   Parmesan
1 egg
1 tbsp Dijon mustard
few drops Worcestershire
   sauce
small bunch parsley, finely
   chopped
oil
½ cup stock
salt and pepper

1   Trim the ends of the spareribs by cutting away about 1½ in of meat from between the ribs and making small slits between the bones at the meaty end so that the rack can be bent around (smooth, bonier side outward) to form a crown.

2   Tie up the crown roast and place in a roasting pan greased with oil.

3   *To prepare the stuffing:* Mix together the chopped ham, pork, egg, parsley and the grated Parmesan.

4   Add the fresh fine breadcrumbs, the mustard, the Worcestershire sauce, a pinch of salt and a little freshly ground pepper. Mix thoroughly with a wooden spoon until well blended and smooth.

5   Spoon the stuffing into the center of the crown roast.

6   Cover the crown loosely with foil and cook in a hot oven (400°F) for 1½ hours. After about 20 minutes pour ½ cup of hot stock into the roasting pan and baste the meat at frequent intervals with the combined juices and stock from the bottom of the pan. When the roast pork is ready to serve, place a small paper crown over each trimmed bone. Garnish with tomatoes and parsley.

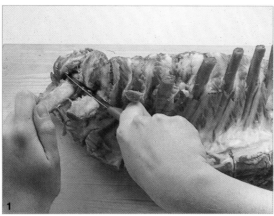

Extra special terrine

Preparation: 1 hour
50 minutes

1¼ cups finely chopped
  or ground pork
1 cup finely chopped or
  ground beef
½ cup finely minced
  chicken
1 cup chicken livers
6 oz fresh pork fat
pinch of thyme
1 bay leaf

1 tablespoon shelled
  pistachio nuts
2 chicken breasts
3 tbsp brandy
3 tbsp Madeira
3 tbsp sherry
2 tbsp butter
salt and pepper

Serve with a little chopped
aspic jelly*; gherkins
and hot French bread.

1 Cut the two chicken breasts into four fillets. Place in a dish with two thirds of the fresh pork fat cut in strips. Pour over the sherry and Madeira and leave for 30 minutes.

2 Melt the butter in a cast-iron skillet, add half the chicken livers and sauté, seasoning with salt and pepper; sprinkle with the brandy and cook until this has evaporated.

3 Blend the remaining diced pork fat and chicken livers until almost a paste. Transfer to a bowl.

4 Remove the skin from the pistachio nuts by pouring boiling water on them and draining immediately; the skins will then rub off. Chop finely and season.

5 Mix the nuts, chicken liver paste, ground pork, beef and minced chicken into a smooth, even mixture.

6 Butter a rectangular terrine, cover the bottom with a layer of the ground meat and nut mixture; place two chicken fillets flat on top of this, together with a few strips of pork fat. Cover with another layer of mixture. Use a piping bag to layer the meat mixture if you like.

7 Arrange the sautéed chicken livers in a line down the center.

8 Cover with another layer of meat mixture and continue layering until all the ingredients have been used. Sprinkle with a little thyme, press the bay leaf into the surface and cover the terrine. Place in a roasting pan half-filled with boiling water (lay a dish towel on the bottom of the roasting pan). Cook for about 1 hour at 375°F. Allow to cool completely before cutting into slices.

Chicken Waterzooi

Preparation: 1 hour
20 minutes

1 3 lb chicken, jointed
1 large onion
3 celery hearts
3 large leeks (green tops
   removed)
6¼ cups veal stock (made
   from raw veal, 1 onion,
   2 small carrots, 1 celery
   stalk, 1 bouquet garni
   and 2 peppercorns)

3 egg yolks
1 tbsp finely chopped
   parsley
3 tbsp grated Parmesan
1 tbsp unsalted butter
1½ tsp cornstarch
salt

This well-known Belgian
dish is traditionally served
on special occasions.
There is an equally
popular version using fish.

200

1   Wash the celery hearts and the trimmed white part of the leeks; dry, then slice into thin strips.

2   Butter a deep, heavy-bottomed enamel pot; place the celery, leeks and chopped onion in the bottom and then place the chicken pieces on top. Cover the chicken with veal stock.

3   Place a circle of buttered wax paper over the pot and seal firmly with the lid. Bring slowly to a boil, lower the heat and simmer gently for an hour. Remove from the heat, take up the chicken pieces and transfer to a heated dish. Cover and keep warm.

4   Beat the egg yolks with the chopped parsley and add the grated Parmesan cheese. Trickle the hot stock from the pot, reserving the vegetables, in a thin stream onto the beaten egg yolks, whisking vigorously.

5   Mix 1½ teaspoons of cornstarch together with a little water or stock and add to the liquid, stirring well. Return this mixture to the heat and simmer gently, stirring constantly, for about 10 minutes or until the sauce has become creamy and thick.

6   Pour the sauce over the chicken pieces and vegetables, arranged in a tureen, and serve immediately.

New Castile chicken with apples

Preparation: 1 hour
45 minutes

1 3½–4 lb chicken
2 apples
juice of 1 lemon
3 tbsp brandy
4 oz sliced bacon or salt
   pork
¾ cup dry white wine
6 tbsp oil
few coarsely ground
   peppercorns
salt and pepper

1   Wash and dry the chicken and season the cavity with a pinch of salt, the coarsely ground peppercorns and the lemon juice.

2   Wash, peel and core the apples, dip in acidulated water if wished to prevent them from discoloring, and cut one in half. Push one half well down into the chicken's cavity, followed by the whole apple and then by the remaining half.

3   Sew up the opening or secure with a skewer; sprinkle the chicken with a little salt and pepper and wrap the slices of bacon or salt pork around it, securing with small skewers.

4   Place the chicken in a casserole dish with the oil and cook in a hot oven at 400°F, turning once or twice so that it browns evenly; after 30 minutes mix the brandy with the wine and pour over the chicken.

5   Continue cooking for another 40–50 minutes or until the meat is tender and the juices run clear when the thigh is pierced with a knife. Baste frequently with the cooking juices and oil.

6   When the chicken is cooked, joint into four pieces and serve at once, garnishing each serving with half an apple.

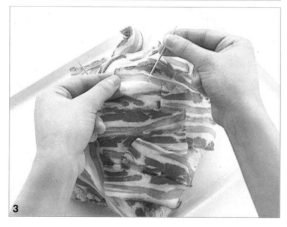

Tunisian chicken

Preparation: 1 hour
30 minutes

1 3½–4 lb chicken
⅔ cup oil
¾ cup pitted green olives
1 tsp anchovy paste (made
   by crushing 1–2
   anchovy fillets into a
   smooth paste)
1½ cups canned tomatoes
1 clove garlic
salt and pepper

1   Wash and dry the chicken and joint into serving pieces.

2   Heat the oil in a large, heavy-bottomed saucepan and brown the chicken pieces all over, turning frequently so that they cook evenly. Season with a little salt and freshly ground pepper. When the chicken is browned, take up the pieces and keep warm.

3   Place the tomatoes in a large, deep skillet, crushing them with a fork to break them up. Stir in the anchovy paste and a couple of spoonfuls of water and simmer for a few minutes.

4   Add the whole peeled garlic clove, then the chicken pieces followed by the olives.

5   Simmer over low heat for 30–40 minutes, stirring now and then, and add a few spoonfuls of hot water if the sauce reduces too rapidly.

6   Remove and discard the garlic; place the chicken portions on a heated serving platter and cover with the sauce. Serve at once.

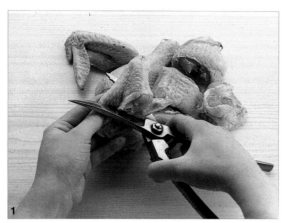

Spicy tomato chicken

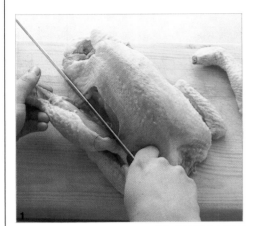

Preparation: 1 hour
30 minutes

1 3½–4 lb chicken
4 large onions
2 large crisp apples
½ cup butter
1 tbsp tomato paste
5 tbsp coconut milk
¾ cup thick cream
2 tbsp lemon juice
pinch of powdered bay
    leaf
pinch of thyme
pinch of cinnamon
1 pint chicken stock
salt and pepper
½ tbsp garam masala

1   Wash the chicken, dry
and cut into serving
pieces.

2   Melt the butter in a
large, heavy-bottomed
saucepan over moderate
heat; add the sliced
onions, the apples,
peeled, cored and
chopped, and the
cinnamon. Fry gently for
5 minutes.

3   Add the chicken
portions and brown for
5 minutes, stirring and
turning frequently.

4   Add the chicken stock,
a pinch of salt, a little
freshly ground pepper, the
thyme and powdered bay
leaf and simmer gently for
30 minutes.

5   Sprinkle in the garam
masala and add the
tomato paste mixed with
the coconut milk.
Continue cooking over
low heat for 8–10
minutes, until the sauce
has reduced and
thickened slightly.

6   Just before serving, stir
in the cream, mixed with
the lemon juice. Reheat
gently and serve with
basmati rice.

Chinese fried chicken

Preparation: 40 minutes

2 spring chicken leg
   quarters
½ beaten egg
4 tbsp cornstarch
few drops sesame oil
   (optional)
oil for frying

To flavor:
¼ tsp salt
2–3 drops soy sauce
1 tsp rice wine
pinch of pepper

1   Wash and trim the chicken legs; dry with paper towels. Using a cleaver, chop through the bone into triangular, bite-size pieces.

2   Mix the beaten egg and the flavoring ingredients together in a bowl and add the chicken pieces.

3   Sprinkle with the cornstarch and mix well. Leave to stand for 5 minutes. If a slightly stronger flavor is preferred, add a few drops sesame oil.

4   Heat plenty of oil in a wok, or deep-fryer, to 350°F.

5   Lower the chicken pieces into the hot oil one by one, working as quickly as possible to ensure even cooking.

6   Adding the chicken to the oil will have lowered the temperature to about 300°F. Maintain this lower temperature by turning down the heat; when the chicken is half done, remove the pieces from the oil and prick them with a skewer to make them cook through more quickly. Lower them into the oil once more.

7   When the chicken is nearly cooked, increase the heat so that the oil is really hot; this will make it easier to drain the chicken so that it does not taste oily.

8   If desired, the flavor can be heightened by stir-frying the drained chicken pieces briefly in another skillet with a few drops of sesame oil and a tablespoon of finely chopped leek.

Curried chicken casserole

Preparation: 1 hour
10 minutes

4 chicken breasts
4 large mushrooms
1 onion
1 clove garlic
1 egg yolk
1 cup dry white wine
¼ cup butter
2 peeled, boiled potatoes
2½ cups milk
½ cup flour
3 tbsp grated Parmesan
1 tbsp curry powder
salt and pepper

1   Peel and slice the onion, dice the chicken breasts; wash, dry and slice the mushrooms.

2   Melt the butter in a deep skillet and gently fry the diced chicken, onion and finely chopped garlic.

3   Pour in the wine and continue cooking until it has evaporated. Season with salt and freshly ground pepper and then take up the chicken, mushrooms and onion with a slotted spoon, and keep warm. Leave the cooking juices in the skillet.

4   Stir the flour into the juices and fat and add the curry powder.

5   Heat the milk to just below boiling point and gradually add to the curry mixture, stirring constantly.

6   Simmer for 5–10 minutes, whisking until the sauce is smooth and creamy.

7   Meanwhile, boil the potatoes and mash into a bowl. Stir in the egg yolk and season with salt and freshly ground pepper, mixing very thoroughly.

8   Butter a deep casserole dish and cover the bottom with one-third of the chicken mixture; cover with half the sauce and sprinkle with half the grated Parmesan cheese. Arrange the rest of the chicken mixture on top and cover with the remaining sauce and cheese. Put a fluted nozzle on a piping bag and spoon the mashed potatoes into the bag; pipe a decorative border around the edge of the dish. Place under a hot broiler until the top is a pale golden brown. Serve straight from the casserole dish while very hot.

Peking duck

Preparation: 5 hours
30 minutes

1 whole duck, weighing
    about 6½ pounds,
    plucked but undrawn
    and with the head left
    on
about 2 inches of the
    white parts of 12
    scallions or leeks
2 tbsp molasses or treacle
24 pancakes*, 4 inches
    in diameter

For the sauce:
4 tbsp sugar
4 tbsp sweet bean paste
2 tbsp sesame oil
(This sauce can be
replaced by hoisin sauce,
which is readily available
from Oriental stores)

1   Wash the duck and cut
off the feet. Make sharp
notches all round the end
of the scallions along the
grain of the stem. Place in
a bowl of iced water for 1
to 2 hours so that the ends
curl into feathery flowers.

2   With a small, sharp
knife pierce the duck's
neck in the front below the
head, making a cut just
large enough to insert a
straw between the skin
and the flesh; blow air
between the skin and flesh
until the whole duck is
expanded; this is vital to
achieve crackly yet
succulent skin.

3   Make a small slit, and
draw the duck.

212

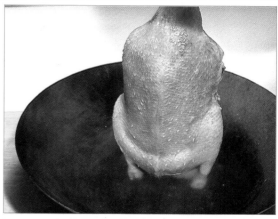

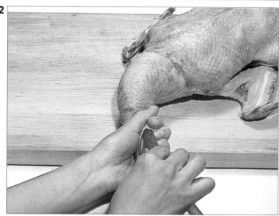

4 Wash the duck inside and out and sew the slit up tightly with kitchen thread or cotton.

5 Trim off the wing tips and hang the duck up over a basin.

6 Pour about 4 cups boiling water over the duck; leave it to dry a little. Combine the molasses with 1 cup boiling water and pour evenly all over the bird; baste well and repeat the process several times. Leave the bird hung up in a warm dry place or in the sun for up to 4 hours or until the skin is completely dry. Cut the head off the duck and place, breast downward, in a large roasting pan and roast in a preheated oven at 400°F for 20 minutes. Turn and continue cooking for a further 20 minutes. Place the roasting pan in a pan of hot water over low heat for a few minutes; then return to the oven for a final 20 minutes' roasting, turning again half-way through.

7 Prepare the sauce: mix the sugar with the sweet bean paste and a generous ½ cup of water. Heat a wok and pour in the sesame oil, add the sauce mixture and cook until it thickens. As an alternative, ready-made hoisin sauce does very well.

8 Carve meat into thin slices. Each person places some meat in a pancake, brushes sauce over it using the scallions, and rolls up the pancake.

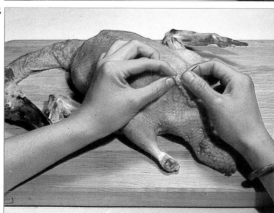

Duck à l'orange

Preparation: 2 hours

1 4 lb duck
½ cup butter
2 oranges
peel of 1 orange
1 cup light stock
1½ tbsp potato flour or
   cornstarch
¾ cup dry sherry
3 tbsp Curaçao
salt and pepper

This simplified version of
the classic French dish
makes a spectacular main
course for a special dinner
party. Garnish with
triangles of bread fried in
butter arranged around
the edge of the serving
dish.

1   Wash the duck and dry well. Place a small piece of butter inside the cavity and rub a little butter over the less fatty parts of the breast; season inside and out with salt and freshly ground pepper. Pierce skin all over with a fork.

2   Place the duck on a rack in a large roasting pan in an oven preheated to 425°F, turning the heat down to 350°F after 15 minutes. A 4 lb duck will take about 1½ hours total cooking time. Alternatively, cook over direct heat in a large deep saucepan. Pierce the breast with the prongs of a fork; when they slide in easily, remove the duck from the roasting pan and keep warm. Reserve the cooking juices.

3   *To prepare the orange sauce*: Pare off the rind of an orange, leaving behind the pith. Blanch in boiling water for a few minutes.

4   Drain off the water, dry the rind and cut into very thin strips; place in a bowl with the Curaçao. Pour the boiling stock into the juices in the roasting pan. Stir in the potato flour or cornstarch mixed with the sherry and cook over high heat until the liquid has reduced by about one third.

5   Add the orange peel and Curaçao and leave to simmer, stirring occasionally, for about 5–10 minutes. Remove from heat.

6   Peel the other oranges, removing all the pith, membrane and seeds from each segment.

7   Cut the duck into pieces and arrange on a heated serving platter; pour over the orange sauce and decorate with the orange segments.

Spanish almond duck

Preparation: 2 hours

1 4 lb duck, liver reserved
flour
½ cup fresh pork fat or
    shortening
2 shallots
1½ cups canned tomatoes
24 almonds
1 clove garlic
small bunch parsley
1 cup dry white wine
salt and pepper

1 Wash the duck, dry thoroughly and joint into serving pieces. Reserve the liver as it is an essential part of this recipe.

2 Melt the finely chopped pork fat in a large, heavy-bottomed saucepan and when it is hot sauté the finely chopped duck's liver for 2 or 3 minutes. Remove with a slotted spoon and keep warm.

3 Sauté the finely sliced shallots until a very pale golden brown, remove these with a slotted spoon and keep warm with the liver.

4 Coat the duck pieces with flour and brown well in the hot fat; season with salt and freshly ground pepper.

5 Add the roughly chopped tomatoes and simmer for about 1 hour, turning and stirring from time to time.

6 Toast the almonds in the oven until light golden brown, then chop them up with the cooked liver, shallots and garlic; place in a bowl and moisten with white wine.

7 Add this mixture to the simmering duck and tomatoes, stir and continue cooking, covered, for about 40 minutes. Serve the duck in its sauce, sprinkled with finely chopped parsley.

217

Stuffed roast turkey

Serves 6

Preparation: 2 hours
30 minutes

1 5–8 lb turkey
2 apples
½ cup ham
small bunch parsley
2 sage leaves
2 shallots
2 cups white bread, crusts
    removed, soaked in
    milk and squeezed out

1 clove
2 eggs
3 tbsp fine breadcrumbs
¼ cup chicken livers
½ cup butter
salt and pepper

For your Thanksgiving or Christmas turkey, a more elaborate stuffing can be used. Instead of ham, use ½ lb button mushrooms; leave out the apples, shallots and sage and substitute two onions, a chopped carrot, a clove of garlic and two small, finely chopped celery stalks. The turkey liver can be used instead of the chicken livers; sauté all these ingredients, finely chopped, in butter and when they are just done, add 2 tablespoons brandy, allow to evaporate and remove from heat. Mix with the eggs, soaked white bread, chopped parsley and a little salt and pepper and then stuff the turkey as above.

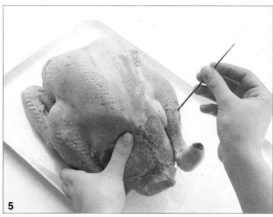

1   Peel, core and chop the apples; sauté them gently in half the butter.

2   Wash and trim the chicken livers; chop finely together with the ham.

3   Transfer to a bowl and add the chopped shallots, sage leaves and parsley. Add the fine breadcrumbs, eggs, the clove, sautéed chopped apple and the white bread moistened with milk; season with salt and a little freshly ground pepper.

4   Mix until the ingredients are well blended. Wash and dry the turkey and season the cavity with salt and pepper; fill with the stuffing.

5   Sew up the opening and place the turkey in a roasting pan. Melt the remaining butter and spread over the breast of the turkey, sprinkle with a little salt and place in the oven, preheated to 400°F.

6   Halfway through the roasting time (allow about 2½–3 hours), cover the turkey with foil and continue roasting, turning the bird from time to time and basting with the juices.

7   When the turkey is done (check that the juices run clear when the thigh is pierced) remove from the oven, carve into serving pieces and serve with the stuffing and the juices from the roasting pan.

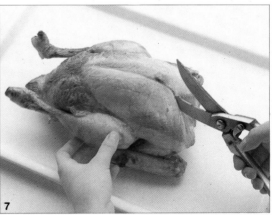

Turkey à la King

Preparation: 1 hour
25 minutes

1¾ lb turkey breast (skin
    removed)
1 medium onion
½ cup butter
3 cups button mushrooms
1 celery stalk
2 red peppers
1 bay leaf
1 clove

½ cup cream
2 egg yolks
1 cup dry white wine
½ cup flour
4 tsp coarse salt
2 peppercorns

Serve with rice

1   Slice the onion and place in saucepan with the celery, bay leaf, clove, peppercorns and salt.

2   Place the turkey breast on top of the vegetables and cover with the wine mixed with 1 pint of water. Bring to a boil and then simmer very gently for 45 minutes.

3   Allow the turkey breast to cool to room temperature in the cooking liquid; drain, dice and set aside. Discard the celery and bay leaf. Reserve stock and onions.

4   Wash and dry the mushrooms and cut into thin slices; sauté for 15 minutes in ¼ cup butter, stirring frequently, then add to the reserved stock containing the onions.

5   Place the peppers under the broiler or hold over a gas burner to scorch the thin outer skin. Peel off the burned skin, remove the stalk, cut open and trim off the pith, removing the seeds. Cut into thin strips and add to the stock.

6   Reserve a little stock to mix with the beaten egg yolks. Melt the remaining butter in a small saucepan, stir in the flour and cook until the roux turns a pale golden brown. Add a little of the stock to dilute, then gradually stir into the stock containing the onions, mushrooms and peppers. Cook for 15 minutes, stirring constantly, and then mix in the cream. After a few minutes reduce the heat (or turn off) and trickle in the egg yolks, beaten with a little of the reserved stock.

8   Mix well and stir in the diced turkey. Arrange the rice on a hot serving platter and spoon the turkey and sauce on top.

Roast goose with chestnuts and apples

Serves 4–6

Preparation: 3 hours

1 4½–8 lb goose
14 oz peeled chestnuts
1½ pints brown stock
pinch of chopped tarragon
3 apples
⅓ cup seedless white
   raisins
2 tbsp potato flour or
   cornstarch
6 tbsp oil
salt and pepper

This German recipe includes one of a great variety of stuffings for roast goose from many parts of the world. You can stuff your bird with sausage meat and beans, sauerkraut and apples or vegetables and fruit. Extra cooking time is always allowed for roasting a stuffed bird.

1   Parboil the chestnuts in 1 pint of stock. Wash, quarter and core the apples. Soak the raisins in warm water.

2   Mix the drained chestnuts with the apple quarters and the well-drained raisins.

3   Wash, dry and season the goose inside and out with salt, freshly ground pepper and tarragon. Fill the cavity with the fruit and chestnut stuffing.

4   Sew up the opening and place the goose in a roasting pan that has been greased with a tablespoon of oil.

5   Place in a hot oven, preheated to 400°F, and roast for about 2½–3 hours. Baste from time to time with a little of the remaining hot stock and turn the bird at intervals.

6   When the goose is cooked, transfer it from the roasting pan onto a heated serving platter. Strain the cooking juices and liquid from the pan into a small saucepan; mix the potato flour or cornstarch with a little cold water, add to the saucepan and cook for about 5 minutes, stirring constantly. Pour over the goose.

Oriental Rock Cornish hens

Preparation: 1 hour
10 minutes

2 Rock Cornish hens,
   cleaned
1 can dried chestnuts
generous ¼ cup butter
¾ cup dry white wine
¾ cup cream
1¼ lb bacon or salted
   smoked belly of pork
1 small onion
1 cup fine fresh
   breadcrumbs
juice of ½ lemon

3 sage leaves, chopped
1 tbsp tomato paste
6 tbsp stock
6 tbsp grated Parmesan
1 bay leaf
scant ¾ cup Marsala
¼ stock cube
1 heaping tsp cornstarch
scant 1 cup oil
nutmeg
salt and pepper

1   Simmer the dried chestnuts for a few minutes then set aside.

2   Chop the onion finely with the bacon and fry in 2 tablespoons butter with the bay leaf.

3   Add the breadcrumbs, grated Parmesan and lemon juice and mix well.

4   Stir in 1 teaspoon tomato paste followed by about two thirds of the drained chestnuts. Crush them into the mixture with a fork. Season with salt, grated nutmeg, pepper and the sage leaves.

5   Cut the hens in half and pound flat with the meat mallet. Heat the oil in a very large skillet and fry each halved hen over high heat for 15 minutes, turning frequently. Season, and moisten with a little white wine.

6   Place each halved hen on a chopping board and cover with a few spoonfuls of the chestnut, cheese and breadcrumb mixture; press one or two of the reserved chestnuts on top. Sprinkle with a little grated Parmesan. Place in the oven (preheated to 350°F) and cook for 10–15 minutes or until golden brown.

7   Make the sauce. Work the cornstarch into the remaining softened butter and stir into the cooking juices in the pan. Stir in the remaining tomato paste mixed with the stock and cook over low heat; when the sauce has thickened slightly, add the Marsala and cream. Crumble the extra stock cube into the sauce and mix well; simmer, stirring constantly, for about 10 minutes. Serve at once, spooning a little sauce on to each plate and placing half a hen on top. Serve any remaining sauce separately.

Pheasant à la georgienne

Preparation: 1 hour
30 minutes

1 plump young hen
  pheasant
12 strips barding fat
  (bacon or salt pork)
20 walnuts
1¾ lb white grapes
¾ cup strained green tea
juice of 2 large oranges
scant ¾ cup Marsala
3 tbsp butter
salt and pepper

1   Wash and dry the pheasant; season the cavity with a little salt and freshly ground pepper.

2   Wrap the barding fat around the pheasant and secure with wooden skewers.

3   Place in a heavy-bottomed casserole with the butter, adding the orange juice and the chopped or coarsely broken up walnuts.

4   Place the grapes in a sieve and crush with a wooden spoon, collecting the juice in a bowl. Add to the casserole together with the Marsala followed by the green tea; cover and simmer for 40 minutes over gentle heat.

5   When cooked, take up the pheasant, remove the barding fat and return to the casserole to brown. Season with a little more salt and freshly ground pepper.

6   When the pheasant has browned, transfer to a heated serving dish and cover with the sauce.

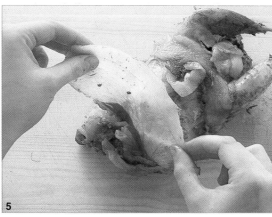

Spanish roast lamb

Preparation: 1 hour
30 minutes

1 3–3¼ lb shoulder of
  baby or milk-fed lamb
4 cloves garlic
½ cup melted fresh pork
  fat
1 lb new potatoes
several sprigs of rosemary
salt and pepper

This delicious way of
presenting lamb, typical of
traditional Spanish
provincial cooking, is both
simple to prepare and
very nourishing. If young
lamb is difficult to find, use
the shank half of a leg
from the youngest,
tenderest lamb available.

1   Peel and crush 3 cloves of garlic and rub into the surface of the lamb or insert into slits in the meat so that it is well flavored.

2   Sprinkle salt and freshly ground pepper on each side of the shoulder before putting it onto a rotisserie spit. Roast in a preheated oven for 40 minutes or until tender at 425°F; place a roasting pan under the lamb to catch the juices and fat as it cooks.

3   At frequent intervals dip a glazing brush into the fat that collects in the roasting pan and baste the shoulder. Once the lamb has started to brown evenly all over, baste every 5–10 minutes, dipping the brush into the melted fresh pork fat. When the lamb is cooked (a rosy pink inside unless you prefer it well done), remove carefully from spit and wrap in foil to keep warm. Turn oven heat down to 350°F.

4   Scrub off the skin of the new potatoes and toss in a large bowl with the chopped rosemary, a crushed clove of garlic and coarse salt.

5   Place the potatoes and rosemary in the hot fat left in the roasting pan, and roast for 30 minutes with the oven at 350°F. Turn the potatoes at least once during cooking.

6   When the potatoes are golden brown, unwrap the lamb and place in the pan; leave in the oven for a few minutes. Serve the lamb on a very hot platter, garnished with a few sprigs of rosemary.

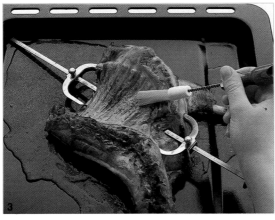

Lamb Provençal

Preparation: 1 hour

1½ lb boned lamb chops
   (or 14 noisettes)
2 zucchini
2 eggplant
2 large but not overripe
   tomatoes
generous pinch mixed
   dried herbs
1½ cups oil
salt and pepper

For the tomato sauce:
12 large ripe tomatoes
½ onion
1 clove garlic
5 tbsp olive oil
salt and pepper

1 If the butcher has not already done so for you, bone the lamb, and slice into thick medallions. Flatten with a meat mallet.

2 Peel lengthwise strips from the zucchini, slice in rounds and fry in half of the oil, preheated until very hot; take up with a slotted spoon and drain on paper towels. Prepare the eggplant in the same way.

3 Heat the remaining oil in the same saucepan and sauté the lamb until well browned on both sides; season with a pinch of salt and freshly ground pepper; take up and set aside on a warm plate.

4 *To prepare the tomato sauce:* Trim, wash and dry the tomatoes; remove the seeds and chop coarsely. Cook slowly in a saucepan with half an onion and a clove of garlic for about 30 minutes. Allow the sauce to reduce and thicken. Pass through a sieve or liquidizer and add a little salt, pepper and olive oil.

5 Grease an oval ovenproof pan with oil and spoon in about ½ cup of the tomato sauce.

6 Arrange the fried vegetables, meat and 2 raw sliced tomatoes in rows across the ovenproof dish, beginning with a row of fried zucchini, then raw tomatoes, followed by fried eggplant and the sautéed lamb. Repeat until all the ingredients have been used up. Sprinkle with the dried herbs.

7 Top with the remaining tomato sauce and bake in a fairly hot oven (350°F) for 20 minutes. Serve immediately.

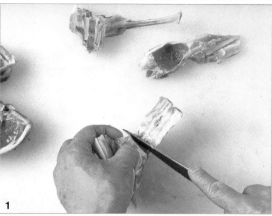

Jellied rabbit mold

Preparation: 1 hour
50 minutes (+ chilling
time)

1 3–3½ lb rabbit
2 pints gelatin (use 1½
   packets powdered
   gelatin dissolved in 1½
   pints light meat stock,
   flavored with ¾ cup
   sherry, cooled but still
   liquid)
1 cup baby carrots, sliced
   into rounds
1 cup baby onions
1 cup small mushrooms
¼ cup pitted black olives

¼ cup pitted green olives
3 tbsp capers
¼ cup butter
1 cup dry white wine
6 gherkins
3 tbsp oil
3 tbsp wine vinegar
1 clove
1 bay leaf
1 clove garlic
1 tbsp chopped chervil
salt and pepper

1   If the butcher has not already done so for you, joint the rabbit into 7–8 pieces (do not use the head). Brown the rabbit in the butter and oil in a heavy-bottomed pot.

2   Season the rabbit pieces with salt and a little freshly ground pepper before adding the onions, sliced mushrooms, clove, bay leaf and garlic.

3   Cook for 15 minutes, then pour in the wine and vinegar. Cover and simmer over very low heat for 1 hour 20 minutes, turning and mixing occasionally with a wooden spatula.

4   *To prepare the savory jelly:* While the rabbit and vegetables are cooking, dissolve the gelatin in the hot broth; when it has dissolved stir in the sherry.

5   Rinse out a large mold with cold water and spoon in enough warm gelatin mixture to cover the bottom. Chill in the refrigerator.

6   When this first layer of jelly has set arrange the cooled pieces of rabbit in the mold, layering them with the slices of raw carrot, chervil, sliced mushrooms, onions and the drained, dried capers.

7   Pour a little gelatin into the mold, chill, and proceed with the next layer. When all the rabbit and vegetables have been set in the jelly, finish off with the remaining liquid gelatin and chill for at least 2 hours.

8   To serve the jellied rabbit, dip the mold almost up to its rim in a large bowl of hot water, cover with the serving plate and then turn the mold upside down on the plate. Garnish with gherkins and black and green olives.

Snails à la Bourguignonne

Preparation: About 4 hours

32 large canned snails
4 carrots
2 medium sized onions
4 shallots
1 clove garlic
1 bouquet garni
coarse salt

For the stuffing:
3 tbsp fine fresh breadcrumbs
1¼ cups softened butter
1 tbsp finely chopped shallot mixed with 1 finely chopped clove garlic
2 heaping tbsp finely chopped parsley
pinch mixed spice
salt and pepper

1   Rinse out the cooking pot and place the drained snails in it; cover with fresh water and sprinkle them with coarse sea salt, allowing about ¼ oz for every 2 pints of water. Slice the carrots, onions and shallots and add to the salted water, together with the peeled, crushed clove of garlic and the bouquet garni. Bring slowly to a boil and simmer for about 3½ hours.

2   Drain the snails in a colander. Cut away the hard, black part at each end of the snail.

3   Wash the shells in warm water and leave to dry on a cloth laid on a cookie sheet. Place in a warm oven with the door open.

4   Work the butter with a fork until it is soft and blend in the very finely chopped shallot, the crushed clove of garlic, the finely chopped parsley, a pinch of salt and freshly ground white pepper. Add a pinch of mixed spice and blend well.

5   Replace the snails in their shells and press the butter mixture into the opening of each shell, smoothing it so that it covers the aperture completely. Sprinkle with fine breadcrumbs and a few drops of melted butter. Place in a hot oven (preheated to 450°F) for 8 minutes.

Eggs and Cheese

Eggs in aspic

Preparation: 1 hour

vinegar
salt
4 eggs
powdered aspic for 2¼
  cups liquid
2 tbsp sherry
1 strip pickled pepper
5-oz can shrimp mousse
½ cup cooked shrimp

1   Bring 4½ cups water,
1 tsp vinegar and a pinch
of salt to a boil in a
saucepan. Simmer gently.
Poach the eggs in the
water for 3 minutes.
Remove with a slotted
spoon and drain on a
teatowel.

2   Prepare the aspic
following the
manufacturer's
instructions and flavor
with 2 tbsp sherry. Leave
to cool.

3   Pour a little aspic into
the bottom of four molds.
Place in the freezer to set.
Cut the pepper into
trefoils and place one on
each set layer of aspic.
Cover with another layer
of aspic and return to the
freezer to set.

4   Spoon a little shrimp
mousse into each mold.
Place an egg on top and
cover with the remaining
aspic. Refrigerate for 2
hours.

5   Dip briefly in hot water
to unmold, and garnish
with shrimp.

Baked eggs with peppers

Preparation: 35 minutes

1 large red pepper
1 large green pepper
3 tbsp oil
1 clove garlic
salt and pepper
1 large onion, chopped
2 tbsp butter
4 eggs
tomato ketchup

1 Hold the peppers on a fork over a flame until the skin blisters and can be peeled off. Seed and cut into strips.

2 Place the oil and whole garlic clove in a skillet and brown. Crush the garlic with a fork, then discard. Add the pepper strips and fry for 2–3 minutes over high heat; lower the heat and cook for about 10 minutes until tender but still firm. Season.

3 Cook the onion in a small saucepan in 2 tbsp butter, adding a few tbsp water so that it does not brown.

4 Divide onion between four gratin dishes. Crack an egg into each, season, and cook in a hot oven (400°F) for 5–8 minutes or until set.

5 Remove from the oven, arrange the peppers around the eggs and pour a ring of ketchup around the yolks.

Fried eggs with tomatoes and mushrooms

Preparation: 15 minutes

¼ oz dried Chinese
   wood-ear fungus
2 eggs
pinch of salt
2 ripe tomatoes, skinned
oil for frying
1 tsp sugar
1 tbsp soy sauce

1   Soak the dried fungus in warm water for 20 minutes, wash well, dry and chop the larger pieces in half.

2   Beat the eggs in a bowl together with a pinch of salt and chop the tomatoes.

3   Heat a wok and pour in 3–4 tablespoons oil. When hot, pour in the eggs.

4   Scoop and turn the omelet mixture, until just set. Remove from the wok; pour in 2 tablespoons oil and heat. Add the chopped tomato and stir-fry lightly. When heated through, return the eggs to the pan, add the fungus, and cook briefly.

5   Sprinkle with the sugar and soy sauce, and serve.

Tea eggs

Preparation: 1 hour

6 eggs
2 tsp tea leaves
1 star anise
1 tsp sugar
¼ tsp salt
1 tbsp soy sauce
2 cucumbers
1 tsp salt
1 tsp hot soybean paste
few drops of sesame oil

1   Hard-boil the 6 eggs and roll against a surface, pressing gently so as to form tiny cracks in the shell.

2   Place in a saucepan of water with the tea, star anise, sugar, salt, and soy sauce. Boil gently for up to 1 hour, turning now and then.

3   Remove from the pan and shell carefully, taking care not to tear the delicate skin immediately under the shell.

4   Slice the cucumbers in half vertically, scoring the skin in a trellis pattern, and cut into small pieces. Place in a bowl and sprinkle with 1 teaspoon salt; when softened, sprinkle with cold water and drain. In a separate bowl mix the soybean paste, the soy sauce, and

the sesame oil; add the cucumber and mix.

5   Arrange the cucumber in a bowl and top with the tea eggs.

Crêpes with radicchio Treviso style

Preparation: 1 hour

2 eggs
¾ cup + 3 tbsp flour
¼ cup + 2 tbsp butter
salt
scant 1 cup milk
2–3 tbsp oil for frying
1 lb radicchio
2 shallots
⅔ cup white wine
pepper
½ cup grated Parmesan

For the white sauce:
¼ cup butter
½ cup flour
4½ cups milk

1 Mix together the eggs and the flour in a bowl. Add 2 tbsp melted butter and a pinch of salt and gradually stir in the milk.

2 Heat a little oil in an 8-in nonstick skillet. Pour in a little of the crêpe mixture and cook quickly on both sides. Remove and set aside.

3 Slice the radicchio and chop the shallots.

4 Melt ¼ cup butter in a skillet and fry the radicchio and shallots for about 15 minutes. Add the white wine, season with salt and freshly ground pepper and cook for another 10 minutes.

5 Prepare the white sauce. Melt the butter in a small saucepan, add the flour and stir for 3 minutes. Gradually pour in the hot milk and cook for 10 minutes, stirring constantly. Season with salt and white pepper.

6 Pour half the sauce into the radicchio mixture and spoon a little of this mixture into the center of each crêpe.

7 Fold each one in four and place in a buttered ovenproof dish.

8 Pour over the remaining white sauce. Sprinkle with Parmesan and bake in a preheated oven at 425°F for 15 minutes.

Shrimp and mushroom crêpes

Preparation: 1 hour

16 crêpes*

For the filling:
1 cup shelled shrimp
1 celery stalk
1 cup mushrooms
½ onion
1 clove garlic
pinch of grated nutmeg
2 sage leaves
5 tbsp olive oil
⅓ cup fresh breadcrumbs
5 tbsp cream
1 tsp lemon juice
½ cup dry vermouth

1 egg yolk
salt and pepper

For the sauce:
3 tbsp butter
¼ cup + 3 tbsp flour
1 pint light stock
½ cup dry white wine
1 egg yolk
1 tbsp tomato paste
salt
white pepper
5 tbsp grated Parmesan
1½ tbsp butter

1   Prepare the crêpes*.
To prepare the filling:
Chop the onion, garlic clove and celery finely and fry gently in the oil until soft.

2   Add the shelled shrimp and sauté for 5 minutes if raw (if cooked, warm through for about a minute); add the washed and chopped mushrooms. Add a little salt and freshly ground pepper, a pinch of grated nutmeg and two chopped sage leaves. Simmer for 10 minutes and then sprinkle in the lemon juice and the breadcrumbs; stir in the vermouth and then the cream and egg yolk.

3   Place equal amounts of this filling on each crêpe and roll up.

4   *To prepare the sauce:*
Melt the butter in a saucepan, stir in the flour and gradually add the hot stock, stirring constantly to prevent any lumps forming. Gradually add the dry white wine and season with salt and white pepper. Remove from the heat and whisk in the beaten egg yolk in a thin stream. Stir in the tomato paste.

5   Place the rolled up crêpes in a shallow ovenproof pan and coat evenly with the sauce.

6   Sprinkle with 5 tablespoons grated Parmesan cheese and dot with butter. Place in a preheated oven at 350°F for 25 minutes until the top is lightly browned.

Crêpes with ricotta and spinach

Preparation: 2 hours

12 crêpes*
1½ cups ricotta cheese
¾ cup cooked chopped
   spinach
2 tbsp grated Parmesan
salt
pepper
nutmeg
few tbsp freshly made
   tomato sauce*
few fresh basil leaves

1   Mix together the crumbled ricotta, spinach, and Parmesan. Season with salt, pepper, and nutmeg.

2   Fill the crêpes with the mixture, roll up and place in a buttered ovenproof pan.

3   Cook at 375°F for 10 minutes. Serve with tomato sauce and garnish with basil.

Crêpe tower

Preparation:
1 hour 20 minutes

9 crêpes*
salt
½ cup + 2 tbsp butter
¾ cup frozen chopped
   spinach
2 cloves garlic
few fresh basil leaves
1 sprig parsley
1¼ cups puréed tomatoes
1¼ cups black olives
1 onion

1   Place 1 tbsp butter in a saucepan and add one whole clove garlic. Add the spinach and a pinch of salt and cook gently for about 15 minutes until the liquid has evaporated. Discard the garlic.

2   Chop together one clove of garlic, the basil and parsley. Cook briefly in 1 tbsp butter, then add the tomatoes. Season, then simmer for 15 minutes until thickened.

3   Pit and chop the olives, reserving three whole ones; chop the onion and fry in 2 tbsp butter; add 1 tbsp flour, then gradually stir in the remaining milk. Season and cook for 10 minutes, stirring occasionally.

4   Line a soufflé dish with foil and place a crêpe in the bottom. Cover with half the spinach, then layer the crêpes alternately with the tomato sauce, chopped olives and white sauce, ending with a crêpe. Refrigerate for 2 hours.

5   Unmold and garnish with the reserved olives and a few onion rings.

Savory filled omelet

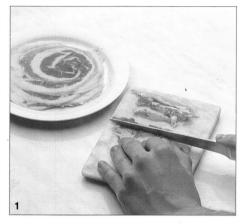

Preparation: 1 hour
15 minutes

2 potatoes
4 oz sliced bacon
1 red onion
2 tbsp oil
6 eggs
1 tbsp grated Parmesan
salt
pepper
1 tbsp butter

1   Peel and dice the potatoes. Cut the bacon into thin strips. Peel and finely chop the onion.

2   Fry the bacon and onion for a few minutes in 2 tbsp oil in a nonstick skillet, then add the potatoes.

3   Season. Cover and cook for 20 minutes, stirring occasionally.

4   Beat the eggs in a bowl and stir in the grated cheese. Season.

5   Melt the butter in a large skillet. Pour the eggs in, and tilt to spread evenly over the bottom. Cook over fairly high heat.

6   Lower the heat and place the potatoes, onion and bacon in the middle. Fold in half, and cook for a few more seconds.

Five-color omelet

Preparation: 20 minutes

2 slices cooked ham
½ bunch scallions
3–4 ounces boiled fresh
    or canned bamboo
    shoots
3 Chinese mushrooms
6 eggs
½ tsp salt
½ tsp sugar
oil for frying

1   Cut the ham into thin strips; chop the scallions.

2   Shred the bamboo shoots and slice.

3   Beat the eggs in a bowl. (Always use *very* fresh eggs when making an omelet.)

4   Mix in the salt and sugar, monosodium glutamate (optional) and beat the eggs briefly but energetically, lifting the mixture to incorporate as much air as possible.

5   Add the ham, scallions, bamboo shoots, and mushrooms and stir well.

6   Heat 2–3 tablespoons oil in a wok; pour the whole omelet mixture into the wok at once, cook until just set, using a spatula or a Chinese scoop or turner to make sure the ingredients are evenly spread throughout the omelet.

7   When the omelet has set on one side, turn it over, dividing it into three portions; then scoop the three portions together again.

8   When the omelet has set into a nicely rounded shape, cover and cook for a very short time, and then serve. The whole of this operation will only take a few minutes.

Chinese eggs with pork

14 oz pork belly
4 Chinese mushrooms
1 leek
2 oz dried shrimp
2–3 tbsp peanut oil
1/3 cup soy sauce
1 tbsp rice wine
1 tsp sugar
pinch five-spice powder
4 eggs

1   Dice the pork belly into 1/2-inch cubes.

2   Chop the mushrooms and leek. Soak the shrimp in water and, when plump, drain, reserving the liquid.

3   Heat the oil in a wok and stir-fry the leek and shrimp.

4   Add the mushrooms and pork belly and stir-fry, add the soy sauce, rice wine, sugar, and five-spice powder. Transfer to a deep saucepan.

5   Add enough stock made up from the shrimp liquid, topping up with water if necessary, to cover all the ingredients.

6   Add the peeled hard-boiled eggs. Cover and cook for about 1 hour.

Cheese ring with herbs

Serves 6

Preparation: 45 minutes

5 oz full fat cream cheese
  with herbs
4 soft processed cheese
  portions (4 oz)
9 oz cream cheese
¼ cup vodka
salt and pepper
1 sprig parsley
1 tbsp butter
few radishes
chives

1   Mash the herb cream cheese in a bowl until creamy. Add the processed cheese portions and mix well.

2   Add the plain cream cheese, continuing to beat, and gradually stir in the vodka. When smooth and well blended season with salt and pepper.

3   Finely chop the parsley. Add to the mixture and stir well.

4   Lightly butter a ring mold and pour in the mixture, pressing firmly with the back of a wooden spoon. Refrigerate for 2 hours.

5   Dip the mold into hot water for a few seconds, then turn out onto a serving dish. Decorate with radishes, parsley, and chives.

Soft cheese bites

Serves 6

Preparation: 15 minutes

4 fresh goat's cheeses
   (approx. 14 oz)
12 slices bread
2 eggs
oil
salt
6 tbsp dried breadcrumbs
4 tbsp grated Parmesan

1   Cut the goat's cheese into equal rounds. From each slice of bread cut two circles slightly bigger than the cheese rings.

2   Beat the eggs with 1 tbsp oil and a pinch of salt; in a separate dish mix the dried breadcrumbs and grated cheese.

3   Dip the cheese rings and bread circles first in beaten egg and then in the breadcrumb mixture. Place a cheese ring on each circle of bread.

4   Place the cheese bites in a heatproof pan and brown under a hot broiler for 5 minutes.

Cheese soufflé

Preparation: 1 hour

¼ cup butter
grated Parmesan
¼ cup + 3 tbsp
   all-purpose flour
1¾ cups milk
salt
nutmeg
3 oz Emmental, grated
4 eggs, separated

1   Butter an 8-inch soufflé dish and sprinkle the inside with grated Parmesan.

2   Melt the butter in a saucepan, then stir in the sifted flour, mixing well to avoid lumps. Cook for 2–3 minutes, then gradually stir in the hot milk. Cook over low heat for 10 minutes.

3   Season with salt and grated nutmeg, then add the Emmental.

4   Cool slightly, then stir in the egg yolks one at a time, mixing in thoroughly.

5   Whisk the egg whites with a pinch of salt until stiff, then gently fold into the sauce using a metal spoon.

6   Pour the mixture into the soufflé dish (it should no more than three quarters fill the dish). Cook in a preheated oven at 400°F for about 30 minutes without opening the oven door. Serve at once before the soufflé collapses.

Fried cheese

Preparation: 50 minutes

10 oz Emmental
1¼ cups puréed tomatoes
2 cloves garlic
oil for frying
salt
oregano
1¾ cups all-purpose flour
scant 1 cup milk
2 eggs, separated

1   Cut the Emmental into wide strips.

2   Prepare the sauce: heat the puréed tomatoes together with the peeled garlic in 5 tbsp oil. Add salt to taste and cook over high heat for 10–15 minutes, adding a generous pinch of oregano.

3   Place the flour in a bowl and gradually work in the milk, beating with a whisk. Add 2 tbsp oil, then stir in the yolks one at a time. Whisk the egg whites until stiff, then, using a metal spoon, fold carefully into the batter.

4   Heat a generous quantity of oil in a skillet. Dip the cheese strips in the batter, using a fork, then deep fry until golden in the oil, which should not be too hot (the batter should not swell up). Drain the cheese strips on kitchen paper and serve hot with the sauce.

Ham and cheese pudding

Preparation: 1 hour
30 minutes

2 tbsp butter
4 tbsp grated Parmesan
16 slices bread
1½ cups milk
8 oz cooked ham, sliced
8 oz mozzarella, thinly
    sliced
salt
6 eggs

1   Butter a high-sided soufflé dish and sprinkle with 2 tbsp Parmesan.

2   Cut the crusts off the bread and briefly dip four, one at a time, in the milk; place them in the soufflé dish to form the bottom layer.

3   Place a layer of ham strips on top; add a few mozzarella slices and a pinch of salt. Repeat the layers, ending with a layer of bread.

4   Beat together the eggs, 4–5 tbsp milk, 2 tbsp Parmesan and a pinch of salt until frothy, then pour into the soufflé dish; pierce the surface with a cocktail stick so that the beaten egg can penetrate to the bottom layers. Leave to stand for 10 minutes.

5   Place a few pieces of butter on the top, then transfer to a preheated oven (350°F) for about 1 hour until golden brown and well risen. Unmold to serve.

Orange or raisin crêpes

For the batter:
⅔ cup milk
⅔ cup light cream
6 tbsp orange liqueur
½ cup all-purpose flour
¼ cup sugar
¼ tsp salt
3 egg yolks
1 egg white
3 tbsp butter

Orange filling:
¼ cup butter
½ cup sugar
1 tsp grated orange peel
1 tbsp brandy
⅔ cup orange juice
orange slices

Raisin filling:
¾ cup raisins
3 tbsp rum
¼ cup butter
½ cup sugar

1   Pour the milk, cream and orange liqueur into a mixing bowl; sift the flour, sugar and salt into the liquid and mix well—there should be no lumps.

2   Beat the egg yolks and white separately and fold into the mixture.

3   Cover and leave for 1 hour.

4   Melt the butter and add to the mixture.

5   Over moderate heat warm a skillet (at least 7 in wide) which has been greased with a film of butter or lard. When the skillet starts to smoke, pour in just enough batter to cover the base. Shake to prevent the crêpe from sticking.

6   When the first side is golden, turn the crêpe over to cook the other side. Repeat the operation until all the batter is used.

7   *For orange crêpes:* beat together the butter, sugar, grated rind and liqueur. Add the orange juice. Cook over low heat until the mixture thickens. Spread each crêpe with a spoonful of the sauce, roll and arrange on a serving dish. Pour the remaining sauce over the crêpes and decorate with slices of orange.

8   *For raisin crêpes:* first soak the raisins in the rum and melt the butter and sugar together in a saucepan. Add the raisins and spirit. When the sauce thickens, remove from the heat. Spread a spoonful of this sauce on each crêpe, roll and arrange on a serving dish; pour the remaining sauce over the crepes and serve.

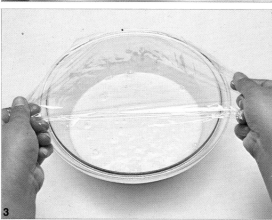

261

Vanilla bavarian cream

2 (¼ oz) envelopes
  unflavored gelatin
2¼ cups milk
1¼ cups sugar
6 egg yolks
1 tsp cornstarch
1 tbsp vanilla sugar
2¼ cups heavy cream
almond or sunflower oil

1   Sprinkle the gelatin into a little hot water in a cup to dissolve it.

2   Reserve a small glass of milk; put the rest of the milk and sugar in a saucepan over low heat.

3   With a balloon whisk, beat the egg yolks, cornflour and vanilla sugar. Add the reserved cold milk. When the milk in the saucepan comes to a boil add it to the egg mixture.

4   Return the mixture to the heat; when it is almost at boiling point, remove and stir in the gelatin. Do not allow to boil.

5   Leave to cool, stirring occasionally.

6   Whip the cream and fold gently into the mixture. Turn into a mold which has been brushed with almond or sunflower oil. Refrigerate for at least 5 hours before serving.

Crème caramel

¾ cup sugar
7 egg yolks
3 egg whites
few drops vanilla essence
2¼ cups milk

1   To make the caramel, heat ¼ cup sugar in a saucepan with a few tsp water, stirring until the syrup turns light brown. Remove from the heat and use immediately.

2   Pour equal quantities of caramel into small molds.

3   Beat the egg yolks and remaining sugar together in a large bowl until thick and creamy.

4   Whisk the egg whites until very stiff and fold into the egg and sugar mixture.

5   Add the vanilla essence to the milk and bring to a boil. Allow to cool a little, then pour into the egg mixture and mix well.

6   Place the molds in a baking tin and fill with water to come half-way up the sides of the molds.

7   Divide the custard between the molds, pouring it through a sieve first to eliminate any lumps.

8   Place the tin in a preheated oven at 325°F for 20–30 minutes or until the custards are firm.

9   Stand them in a cool place for several hours or overnight.

Baked cheesecake

For the pastry:
1 cup all-purpose flour
½ cup sugar
½ tsp salt
½ cup butter
1 egg

For the filling:
10 oz cream cheese
2 eggs
3 tbsp melted butter
¼ cup all-purpose flour
¼ cup sugar
½ tsp vanilla extract
½ tsp salt
1 tsp grated orange peel
½ cup whipping cream
2 tbsp sugar

For the glaze:
1 egg yolk
2 tbsp confectioner's sugar
1–2 tbsp water

1   Preheat oven to 400°F. In a medium bowl, combine flour and salt. Cut in butter until pieces are size of small peas. Add 3 tablespoons water; toss with a fork until all flour is moistened and mixture begins to form a ball. Add more water to crumbs in bottom of bowl, if necessary. Gather dough into a flat ball. Roll out to a 12-inch circle.

2   Fit pastry into a 10-inch fluted pan, pressing to side and bottom of pan. Do not stretch.

3   Prick lightly with a fork.

4   In a large bowl, beat together cream cheese, eggs and butter.

5   Sift flour gradually into cheese mixture. Blend well. Add vanilla and orange peel.

6   In a separate bowl, whip the cream, gradually adding the sugar.

7   Fold whipped cream carefully into the cheese mixture.

8   Pour cheese mixture into pastry-lined pan; smooth top. To make glaze, combine egg yolk, sugar and water. Glaze top of cheesecake lightly. Bake 20 minutes or until golden brown. Makes 1 (10-inch) cheesecake.

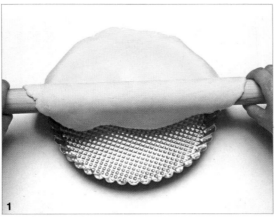

Vegetables

Ravioli filled with mushrooms

Preparation: 1½ hours

1–1¼ lb ravioli
salt
¼ cup butter
4 leaves fresh sage
2–3 sprigs fresh thyme
¾ cup grated Parmesan

For the pasta:
2¼ cups flour
3 eggs, salt

For the filling:
8 oz mushrooms
3 tbsp butter
1 clove garlic
salt
⅔ cup ricotta
1 tsp chopped fresh
  parsley
2 tbsp grated Parmesan
black pepper
1 egg white

1   Rinse, dry and cut the mushrooms into strips.

2   Melt 3 tbsp butter in a skillet. Add the mushrooms, minced garlic and a pinch of salt and cook until the mushrooms are tender.

3   Mix together in a bowl the ricotta, mushrooms, chopped parsley and Parmesan. Sprinkle with freshly ground black pepper and stir well.

4   Prepare the pasta* and cut into 2-in squares using a pastry wheel.

5   Roll the filling into little balls and place one in the center of each square of pasta. Brush the edges with water or egg white and fold over to form a triangle. Press the edges firmly together.

6   Put into boiling salted water and cook for 5 minutes or until *al dente*. Drain and serve in heated dishes.

7   Meanwhile, melt ¼ cup butter in a small skillet and soften the sage leaves and thyme.

8   Sprinkle the ravioli with grated Parmesan and pour over the strained butter.

Fazzoletti with asparagus

Preparation: 1 hour
10 minutes

8 oz fazzoletti
12 oz small green
   asparagus
salt, 1 tbsp olive oil
4 tbsp grated Parmesan
pepper
12 squash flowers
1 small zucchini
¼ cup + 2 tbsp butter

For the pasta:
1¾ cups flour
2 eggs
salt

For the sauce:
¼ cup butter
¼ cup + 3 tbsp flour
1 cup + 2 tbsp milk
nutmeg

1 Trim and rinse the asparagus. Cut off the green tips and cook the stems in boiling salted water for about 15 minutes.

2 Drain the stems and purée in a blender.

3 Cook the asparagus tips in boiling salted water for about 10 minutes.

4 Prepare a sheet of pasta* and cut into eight 4-in squares. Cook the fazzoletti in plenty of boiling salted water for 3–5 minutes, adding 1 tbsp oil to prevent them from sticking together.

5 Melt ¼ cup butter in a small saucepan, add the flour and stir for 1 minute. Add the hot milk and a pinch of nutmeg and cook for about 15 minutes.

6 Add the asparagus purée and season lightly with salt.

7 Place a fazzoletto in each of four dishes; arrange the asparagus tips on top, pointing outward. Sprinkle with grated Parmesan and pepper. Place three squash flowers on top and cover with a little sauce. Cover with a second square of pasta.

8 Garnish each dish with a few slices of zucchini, sautéed in 2 tbsp butter, and two asparagus tips. Transfer to a preheated oven, at 325°F, for a few minutes. Pour 1 tbsp melted butter over each dish before serving.

Tortelli with pumpkin

Preparation: 1¾ hours

1¾ lb pumpkin
2 oz macaroons (amaretti)
3½ oz sweet fruit pickle
    (Cremona mustard)
6 tbsp grated Parmesan
nutmeg
salt and pepper
½ cup butter

For the pasta:
2¼ cups flour
3 eggs
salt

1   Cut the pumpkin into slices and discard the seeds. Remove the rind and bake the slices in the oven for 20 minutes.

2   Press the pumpkin through a fine sieve with the back of a wooden spoon.

3   Crush the macaroons and mix with the minced sweet fruit pickle, 2 tbsp grated Parmesan and a pinch of nutmeg. Season with salt and pepper and stir well.

4   Prepare a sheet of pasta dough* and roll out into two layers. Using a knife score the bottom sheet into twenty 4-in squares. Place a ball of filling in the center of each square.

5   Cover with the second sheet of dough; press round the edges of each square to seal, then cut out the tortelli with a pastry wheel.

6   Cook the tortelli in boiling salted water for 2 minutes.

7   Remove them one at a time from the saucepan, using a slotted spoon. Drain and place on warmed plates.

8   Sprinkle with grated Parmesan and spoon over the melted butter.

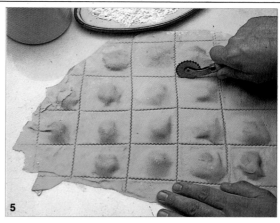

Spinach gnocchetti with leeks and beans

Preparation: 2 hours
40 minutes (+ 12 hours
for soaking the beans)

⅔ cup cannellini beans
salt and pepper
10 oz potatoes
8 oz spinach
2 egg yolks
1 cup flour
nutmeg
8 leeks
¼ cup + 3 tbsp butter
4 fresh basil leaves
4 fresh sage leaves
1 cup white wine
6 tbsp meat stock
   (preferably veal)

1 Soak the beans in cold
water for 12 hours; drain,
then cook in boiling salted
water for 1¼ hours. Skin
and boil the potatoes, then
mash them.

2 Cook the rinsed
spinach for 5–7 minutes
until tender. Drain well
and mince in a food
processor.

3 Mix the chopped
spinach with the potatoes;
add the egg yolks, flour, a
pinch of nutmeg and salt
and work together until
well blended.

4 Break off pieces of the
mixture and roll into
sausages the thickness of
your finger; cut into
gnocchetti.

5 Cut the leeks into
1½-in pieces and fry
gently in a skillet in ¼ cup
butter. Add the basil, sage
and white wine and
simmer gently. Add the
beans with a little of their
cooking liquor and the
meat stock. Simmer for a
few minutes.

6 Cook the gnocchetti in
boiling salted water for
2–3 minutes. Drain,
season with pepper and
sauté briefly in the
remaining butter. Serve in
very hot dishes with the
beans and leeks and a little
of the cooking liquid from
the vegetables.

Gazpacho

Preparation: 40 minutes

2 slices bread
½ cup red wine vinegar
1 small cucumber
1 red pepper
2 cloves garlic
1 large onion
1 cup olive oil
1½ lb ripe plum tomatoes
salt
pepper

To serve:
1 red pepper, diced
1 cucumber, diced
croûtons
12 small onions
2 hard-boiled eggs

1   Soak the bread in the vinegar for a few hours.

2   Into a blender place the soaked bread, the peeled and roughly chopped cucumber, 1 seeded and chopped red pepper, the garlic, the peeled and sliced onion, ½ cup olive oil and 2¼ cups water. Blend until smooth and then pour into a bowl.

3   Skin and seed the tomatoes then mash to a pulp. Add to the puréed vegetable mixture, season with salt and pepper and refrigerate.

4   Serve the gazpacho with ice cubes, and bowls of diced red pepper, diced cucumber, small onions, hard-boiled eggs and croûtons.

Vichyssoise

Preparation: 1 hour
(+ chilling time)

6 large leeks
8 oz potatoes
¼ cup butter
white pepper
salt
1 bouquet garni
1 cup light cream
chicken stock
chives

1   Trim the leeks and cut the white part into rings, keeping some of the green for garnish. Peel and dice the potatoes.

2   Melt the butter and sauté the leeks without letting them brown. Add the potatoes and stir well to coat. Season with pepper.

3   Cook for a few minutes, then add 6¼ cups water. Add salt to taste and the bouquet garni and bring to a boil. Lower the heat and simmer for about 40 minutes, half covered.

4   Purée in a blender, return to the saucepan and add the cream and a little chicken stock as required. Reheat gently but do not allow to boil. Cool then refrigerate for at least 1 hour.

5   Serve chilled, garnished with chopped chives and a few green leek rings.

Country-style chickpea soup

Preparation: 3 hours

2¼ cups chickpeas
14 oz beets
½ onion
4 tbsp oil
7 oz pork rind, chopped
1 cup freshly made tomato
   sauce*
salt and pepper
2 tbsp grated Parmesan
few slices toasted bread

1   Soak the chickpeas for 12 hours. Drain, then bring to a boil in fresh, unsalted water. Simmer for 2 hours.

2   Trim the beets and shred the leaves, reserving the stalks. Fry the chopped onion in the oil in a saucepan, then add the pork rind, tomato sauce, beet leaves, and salt to taste; cook over medium heat for 1 hour, adding 6¼ cups water.

3   Add the chickpeas and the chopped beet stalks. Cook for another hour.

4   Serve sprinkled with grated Parmesan and black pepper. Accompany with slices of toasted bread.

Italian minestrone

Preparation: 1 hour
40 minutes

2 medium carrots
2 stalks celery
1 head lettuce
4 leaves Savoy cabbage
½ cauliflower
2 potatoes
5 tbsp oil
salt and pepper
2 tbsp tomato purée
2 bouillon cubes
1 bunch parsley
sprig rosemary
2 cloves garlic
¾ cup small pasta (e.g. *ditalini*)
2 tbsp grated Parmesan

1   Shred the lettuce and cabbage. Cut the cauliflower into florets. Peel and slice the carrots; chop the celery and dice the potatoes.

2   Heat the oil in a large saucepan over low heat, then sauté the vegetables for 10 minutes, stirring occasionally. Season with pepper; add the tomato purée and 6¼ cups water.

3   Crumble the bouillon cubes into the soup; adjust the seasoning and cook for about 1¼ hours.

4   Chop the herbs and the peeled garlic. Add to the soup, together with the pasta, and cook until *al dente*. Add the Parmesan before serving.

Stuffed onions

Preparation: 2 hours

1 oz dried mushrooms
4 large white onions
1 red pepper
3 tbsp oil
salt and pepper
2 tbsp breadcrumbs
1 cup grated Emmental
   cheese
3 tbsp butter

1   Soak the mushrooms in warm water for 20 minutes. Squeeze out and chop.

2   Peel the onions, cover with water and boil for 15 minutes. Drain, cool, then cut off the top; scoop out and reserve the middle. Dice the pepper.

3   Chop the middles of the onions and sauté in the oil. Add the red pepper and the mushrooms. Season. Cover and simmer for 10 minutes. Remove from the heat and add the breadcrumbs. Stir.

4   Stuff the onions with the mixture and place in a buttered ovenproof pan. Sprinkle with grated Emmental and melted butter. Bake at 350°F for 50 minutes, covering with foil if they begin to brown too much. Serve hot.

Vegetable molds

Preparation: 1 hour

2 carrots
2 zucchini
1 large eggplant
1 large red pepper
½ cup grated Parmesan
¼ cup milk or cream
2 bunches fresh basil
9 oz plum tomatoes (or
    canned)
3 eggs
7 tbsp oil
butter
salt and pepper

1   Dice the carrots. Cut the zucchini and eggplant into medium pieces. Using a fork, hold the pepper over a flame until the skin blisters, then rinse under cold running water and rub off the skin. Chop.

2   Boil a small amount of water in two separate saucepans. Add the carrots to one and the zucchini and eggplant to the other, and cook for about 15 minutes, adding the pepper to the carrots for the last few minutes. Drain, cool, then place in a blender with the milk (or cream), 4–5 tbsp oil, the eggs and grated cheese. Blend until smooth. Add salt to taste, then divide the mixture between four buttered molds. Place in a *bain marie* and bake at 375°F for about 20 minutes.

3   Peel and chop the tomatoes, blend with the basil, and a few tbsp oil. Season.

4   Remove the molds from the oven and allow to cool. Unmold on to serving dishes on a layer of tomato sauce. Serve the remaining sauce separately.

281

Stuffed cabbage leaves

Preparation: 1 hour
30 minutes

10 oz potatoes, peeled
8 Savoy cabbage leaves
salt
¼ cup butter
½ cup milk
¼ cup grated Parmesan
pepper
nutmeg
2 oz cooked ham
1 bunch parsley
1 egg
1 tbsp breadcrumbs

1   Boil the potatoes for
20 minutes. Cut the
central rib away from the
cabbage leaves and
discard.

2   Cook the cabbage
leaves in salted water for 5
minutes, then dry on a
teacloth.

3   Mash the potatoes.

4   Add half the butter, the
milk and half the cheese.
Season with salt, pepper
and grated nutmeg. Stir
over low heat until the
mixture is quite dry, then
remove from the heat and
add the chopped ham and
parsley. Stir in the egg and
breadcrumbs; mix well
and adjust the seasoning.

5   Place a cabbage leaf
on a chopping board,
overlapping the edges of
the cut, and place one
eighth of the mixture in
the center.

6   Fold the edges of the
leaf over toward the
center to make a parcel.
Fill all the leaves and place
in a buttered ovenproof
pan. Sprinkle with the
remaining melted butter
and cheese and cook at
400°F for 15–20 minutes.

Zucchini with tasty sauce

Preparation: 40 minutes

4 oz parsley
3 anchovy fillets in oil
2 cloves garlic
1 tbsp vinegar
½ cup olive oil
salt and pepper
1 hard-boiled egg
6 medium zucchini
flour
oil for frying

1   Chop the parsley, anchovy fillets and garlic. Mix in a bowl, adding the vinegar, olive oil, salt and pepper.

3   Chop the hard-boiled egg finely and add to the sauce.

4   Slice the zucchini lengthwise and coat lightly in flour. Fry in plenty of hot oil until just brown. Drain on kitchen paper.

6   Arrange in layers on a serving dish, sprinkling each layer with a little salt and some sauce, and chill for 2–3 hours before serving.

Leeks with herb sauce

Preparation: 1 hour

1½ lemons
3 parsley stalks
2 shallots
12 white peppercorns
1 tbsp cumin seeds
6 coriander seeds
1 bay leaf
8 medium leeks
3 egg yolks
½ cup yoghurt
salt
1 tsp mustard
few drops Worcestershire
    sauce
few chives

1   Place 1⅛ cups water and the juice of 1 lemon in a saucepan with the parsley, the chopped shallots, peppercorns, cumin, coriander and bay leaf; boil for a few minutes.

2   Cut the leeks to equal lengths and rinse well. Place in a saucepan and pour over the filtered stock. Cover and cook over low heat for 15 minutes.

3   In a bowl beat the egg yolks, yoghurt and juice of ½ lemon. Cook in a *bain marie* for 10–12 minutes, stirring and adjusting the seasoning as necessary. Remove from the heat and stir in the mustard, Worcestershire sauce and a sprinkling of pepper.

4   Drain the leeks; arrange on a serving dish and cover with the sauce. Garnish with chopped chives.

Cucumber and crisp cabbage salad

Preparation: 1 hour

2 small cucumbers
2 tsp salt
3–4 cabbage leaves

For the sauce:
1 tsp soy sauce
1 tbsp hot black bean
　paste (available from
　Oriental stores)
few drops of sesame seed
　oil

1　Trim the ends off the cucumbers diagonally and slice diagonally into thin pieces. Sprinkle the slices with 1 tsp salt and leave to stand for a few minutes.

2　Cut out the hard ribs of the cabbage, wash and then cut into small pieces 1½–2 in long; sprinkle with 1 tsp salt and leave to stand.

3　When the cucumber and cabbage slices have softened a little, rinse off the salt and drain.

4　Mix all the sauce ingredients thoroughly together in a bowl, add the cucumber and cabbage pieces, stir well and leave the vegetables to absorb the sauce before serving.

Bamboo shoots with spinach and mushrooms

approximately 1 lb fresh spinach
3½ oz bamboo shoots
4–5 Chinese winter (black) mushrooms
oil for frying
1 tsp salt
1 cup water
1 tbsp oyster sauce
few drops of sesame oil
1 tsp cornstarch dissolved in 2 tsp water

1   Wash the spinach; pat dry and chop.

2   Boil the bamboo shoots until tender and slice thinly.

3   Soak the mushrooms in water for 20 minutes, if they are dried; remove the stems and cut the larger caps in half.

4   Heat 2 tablespoons oil in a wok, stir-fry the spinach briefly and then add the salt and water. Cover and cook over low heat until tender; drain.

5   Clean the wok and heat 2 tablespoons of fresh oil; when very hot, add the bamboo shoots and the mushrooms and stir-fry.

6   When nearly done, add the spinach, stock and oyster sauce, finishing with a few drops of sesame oil.

7   Cover and cook for 2 to 3 minutes. Thicken the sauce by stirring in 1 teaspoon cornstarch mixed with 2 teaspoons water.

Vegetable pie

Preparation: 1 hour 10 minutes

8 oz frozen puff pastry
4 oz carrots
2 small onions
¼ cup butter
1 cup peas
⅓ cup spinach, cooked and chopped
salt
1½ cups ricotta
2 eggs
¼ cup grated Parmesan
½ cup milk
flour

1   Thaw the pastry at room temperature. Boil the carrots and slice the onions.

2   Fry the onion in ¼ cup butter for 5 minutes, then add the peas, carrots and spinach. Season.

3   Transfer to a bowl; add the crumbled ricotta, eggs, grated cheese and milk. Season again.

4   Divide the pastry in two; roll out and cut two circles, one slightly larger than the other. Butter and flour a springform pie pan and line with the larger pastry circle. Prick the surface.

5   Pour in the filling and cover with the second pastry circle.

6   Cook in a hot oven (400°F) for 40 minutes.

Fennel au gratin

Preparation: 50 minutes

2 lb fennel
salt
6 oz cooked ham
6 slices cheese
1 tbsp butter
3 tbsp grated Parmesan
1 tbsp chopped parsley
2 tbsp butter
¼ cup flour
1 cup milk
salt
pepper
pinch nutmeg

1   Cut each fennel bulb lengthwise into eight. Cook in boiling salted water for 5 minutes. Cut the ham and cheese into strips.

2   Butter a baking pan and arrange alternate strips of fennel, ham, and cheese in a wheel. Sprinkle with a little grated cheese and chopped parsley.

3   Melt the butter in a saucepan. Stir in the flour and cook for 1 minute. Gradually stir in the milk, mixing well over low heat until thick. Season with salt, pepper, and nutmeg. Pour the sauce over the fennel, sprinkle with the remaining cheese and cook at 400°F for about 25 minutes until crisp and brown.

Baked eggplant

Preparation: 1 hour
30 minutes

2 large eggplant
salt and pepper
2/3 cup ground beef
2 oz pork
2 oz sausage
1 egg yolk
1 tbsp chopped parsley
6 tbsp grated Parmesan
oil for frying
1/4 cup butter

1   Slice the eggplant. Sprinkle with salt and leave in a colander for 1 hour to drain away the bitter juices. In a blender or food processor blend the ground beef, pork and skinned sausage. Transfer to a bowl and mix in the egg yolk, chopped parsley and 2 tbsp Parmesan. Season.

2   Fry the eggplant in plenty of oil until tender. Drain on kitchen paper.

3   Place a little meat mixture on eight eggplant slices then cover each one with another slice, pressing lightly. Place in a single layer in a buttered ovenproof pan. Sprinkle with 4 tbsp Parmesan and a few pieces of butter. Bake at 400°F for 35 minutes.

Savory potato croquettes

Preparation: 1 hour
10 minutes

2 lb potatoes
salt
1 medium onion
oil
2 cups shelled peas
½ bouillon cube
3 tbsp butter
4 eggs, separated
4 tbsp grated Parmesan
2 oz cooked ham
flour

1   Boil and mash the potatoes. Chop the onion and fry briefly in 2 tbsp oil. Add the peas and the crumbled bouillon cube; cover and simmer over low heat for 20 minutes, stirring occasionally and adding a little water as necessary.

2   Stir the butter into the cooled potatoes, 4 egg yolks, the Parmesan, chopped ham, peas and a pinch of salt. Mix well.

3   Turn the mixture on to a work surface and shape into croquettes.

4   Beat 2 egg whites with 1 tbsp oil. Coat the croquettes lightly with flour, then dip in the egg white mixture. Fry a few at a time in plenty of hot oil.

Potato bake

Preparation: 1 hour

2 lb potatoes
6 tbsp oil
⅓ cup grated Parmesan
½ cup grated Emmental
   cheese
salt
pepper
2 tbsp butter

1   Peel the potatoes then grate them using a hand grater or food processor. Mix in a bowl with the oil, ¼ cup grated Parmesan and ¼ cup grated Emmental. Season.

2   Butter an ovenproof baking pan and pour in the potato mixture. Smooth the surface and sprinkle with the remaining cheese and a few pieces of butter.

3   Bake at 425°F for about 30 minutes until golden brown.

Carrot ring cake

For the dough:
½ cup carrots
¼ cup sugar
3 egg yolks
⅓ cup all-purpose flour
½ cup ground almonds
1 tsp grated lemon peel
1 tbsp lemon juice
2 tbsp orange liqueur
butter to grease and flour
   to dust mold

For the buttercream:
4 tbsp confectioner's sugar
¼ cup butter
1 egg yolk
1 tbsp kirsch

This recipe is a variation of one of the most famous types of carrot cake, made in the state of Aargau in Switzerland. It is sometimes covered with chocolate icing. The Aargau carrot cake is covered with kirsch-flavored icing and is decorated with chopped, toasted almonds, then sprinkled with confectioner's sugar.

1   Butter and flour a ring mold.

2   Peel and grate the carrots.

3   Place the sugar, egg yolks and flour in a basin over hot water and whisk until the mixture thickens.

4   Remove from the heat and stir in the carrots, ground almonds, grated lemon peel and lemon juice.

5   Whip the egg whites until stiff.

6   Fold carefully into the carrot mixture.

7   Pour half the mixture into the mold. Prepare the kirsch-flavored buttercream* and spread over the surface, then cover with the remaining mixture.

8   Bake in a preheated oven at 350°F for 45 minutes. Unmold and brush the top with Cointreau. Decorate with Chantilly cream*.

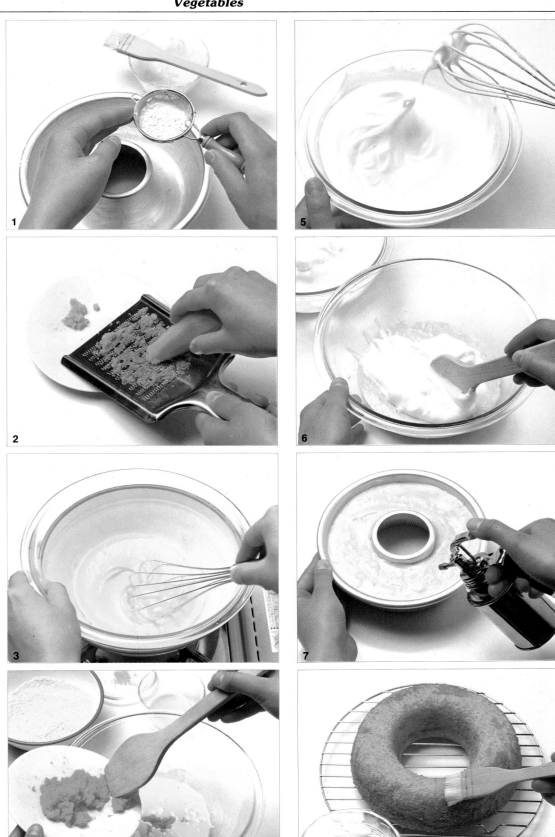

Fruit

Hawaiian fruit salad

½ fresh pineapple
2 bananas
juice of ½ lemon
2 kiwi fruit
1 mango
3 or 4 lettuce leaves
1 orange or tangerine,
    peeled, segmented
10 maraschino cherries,
    drained
2 tbsp sugar

Orange cream:
½ cup orange juice
¼ cup sugar
1 egg yolk, beaten
¾ cup whipping cream

Fruit salads are often served with whipping cream or sweet liqueur, such as Marsala, maraschino or kirsch. This one has an unusual cream dressing. Some more elaborate fruit salads can be garnished with yogurt, cream cheese, chopped toasted nuts or whole nuts, such as pine nuts.

1   Drain off the juice from the pineapple half.

2   Remove the hard core from the half pineapple. Cut all round the flesh of the pineapple so that it can be removed in chunks with a teaspoon.

3   Lay the empty pineapple half cut side down on a cloth to drain the fruit of the remaining juice.

4   Peel and slice the bananas and sprinkle with the lemon juice.

5   Peel and slice the kiwi fruit.

6   Peel the mango, remove the stone and cut the fruit into pieces.

7   Arrange the lettuce leaves in the pineapple half and fill with the drained fruit pieces; add the mandarins in segments and the cherries. Sprinkle with sugar.

8   To make the orange cream, place the orange juice in a saucepan, add the sugar and dissolve over low heat. Remove from the heat. Beat the egg yolk in a basin with a metal whisk and add to the orange mixture. Stir over very low heat until the custard thickens. Allow to cool completely. Whip the cream and stir into the orange sauce. Chill the cream in the refrigerator and pour over the fruit salad just before serving.

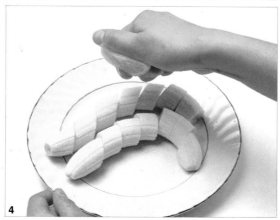

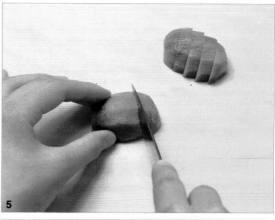

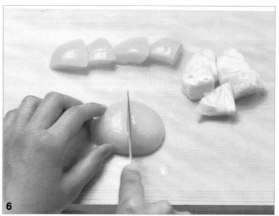

Baked apple

Serves 1

1 large baking apple
1 tbsp apricot jam or
  peach jam
1 shortbread cookie or
  macaroon, crumbled
1 tsp butter
sliced almonds
1 tsp sugar
⅓ cup Marsala or port

1   Wash and dry the apple. Remove the core. With a sharp knife cut a circle right round the apple. Place in a buttered baking pan.

2   Mix the jam with the crumbled cookie and stir until smooth; fill the center of the apple with this mixture.

3   Dot the top of the apple with butter and with sliced almonds.

4   Sprinkle the apple with the sugar; this will form a crust when the apple is cooked.

5   Pour the Marsala or port into the baking pan and bake the apple in the top part of the oven, preheated to 350°F for 30 minutes.

Turkish oranges

Serves 6

6 oranges
water
1¾ cups sugar
2 cloves

1   Peel the oranges thinly, taking care not to cut away the pith with the rind. Cut the peel into very thin strips.

2   Cover the peel with cold water, bring to a boil and drain when the peel is tender.

3   Place the sugar, ½ cup of water and the cloves in a saucepan and heat gently until the mixture begins to caramelize.

4   Add the shredded peel and ¼ cup water and stir until the peel is coated with syrup. Leave to cool slightly.

5   Carefully spoon the syrup and caramelized peel over the oranges, turning them so that they are evenly covered with syrup and peel.

6   Chill the oranges in the refrigerator for several hours. Before serving, quarter the oranges from top to bottom.

Glazed fresh fruit

glacé icing or
  liqueur-flavored glacé
  icing*
fresh fruit of choice

Choose your liqueur
according to the fruit you
are using. For example,
use brandy with grapes
and kirsch, cherry brandy
or maraschino with
cherries.

1 Wash the fruit and dry
carefully with a clean
cloth.

2 Dip the fruit into the
glaze and allow the glaze
to harden.

Almond-filled dried fruit and nuts

almond paste*
food coloring (optional)
dried dates, prunes,
    apricots, peaches or
    other dried fruit
halved walnuts, pecans,
    almonds or other nuts

1   Remove the stones from the dates and prunes, cutting the fruit in half or leaving the two halves slightly joined. Fill with the almond paste.

2   For the nuts, divide the kernel in half and sandwich the two halves together with the almond paste (plain or colored with food coloring). You can also dip stuffed dried fruit and nuts into melted chocolate and allow the chocolate to harden.

Banana crêpes

Preparation: 1 hour
(+ 2 hours for resting the batter)

4 ripe bananas
1 lemon
1 envelope (1 tsp) vanilla
   sugar
⅔ cup brandy
2 eggs
salt
1 cup flour
1⅛ cups milk
¼ cup butter
1 tbsp sugar

1   Peel the bananas and cut in half lengthwise. Sprinkle with lemon juice.

2   Mix together the vanilla sugar and ⅓ cup brandy. Stir well. Pour over the bananas; leave to stand.

3   Beat the eggs in a bowl with a pinch of salt; gradually stir in the flour and then the cold milk. Add 1 tbsp melted butter and 2 tbsp brandy. Leave to stand for 2 hours, then make 8 crêpes.

4   Wrap each half banana in a crêpe and place on a serving dish. Heat ⅓ cup brandy with 1 tbsp sugar in a small saucepan. Flame and pour over the crêpes.

Fruit salad and cream

2 lb assorted fresh or
   canned fruit
½ cup sugar
few drops vanilla extract
juice of 1 lemon
2–3 tbsp rum or
   maraschino
2¼ cups light cream
½ cup chopped dried fruit
¼ cup chopped nuts

1   Wash, drain and peel
the fresh fruit. Slice the
fresh and the canned fruit.

2   Place, together with
the dried fruit, in a large
serving bowl.

3   Mix together the sugar,
vanilla essence, lemon
juice and liqueur. Pour
over the fruit salad and
stir.

4   Pour over the cream
and scatter the chopped
nuts on top.

5   Leave to stand in a
cool place for several
hours before serving.

Melon Portuguese

1 2-lb cantaloupe or
  honeydew melon
¼ cup sugar
½ tsp ground cinnamon
1 cup white port
Chantilly cream*

1   With the stalk
uppermost, cut a zigzag
ring round the melon and
remove the top. Scoop
out the seeds.

2   Remove the flesh from
the melon using a melon
scoop.

3   Replace the balls of
melon in the shell; add
sugar and cinnamon and
leave to stand for 15
minutes.

4   Add the port and place
in the refrigerator for 1
hour.

5   Serve with Chantilly
cream. This fruit salad is
served in the melon shell.
It can be prepared in
various ways. Add
blueberries and a
sprinkling of pistachios,
use kirsch or maraschino
liqueur instead of port
wine, or add other mixed
fruits to melon. Top with
vanilla ice cream and
brandy. Or add pineapple,
bananas and kirsch.

Peach Melba

2 pints fresh raspberries or
   1 (8-oz) jar seedless
   raspberry jam
2–4 tbsp warm water
1 cup confectioner's sugar
¼ cup lemon juice
⅛ tsp vanilla extract
2–3 tbsp raspberry liqueur
   or other sweet liqueur
6 fresh peaches, peeled,
   halved or 12 canned
   peach halves
1 cup granulated sugar
2 cups water
1 quart vanilla ice cream

1   Purée the raspberries with the water in a blender. If you are using jam, heat it gently with a little water.

2   In a large bowl mix together the raspberry purée, sugar, lemon juice, vanilla essence and liqueur. Place in the refrigerator for 1 hour.

3   Place a layer of ice cream in the bottom of 6 glasses or dishes; place 2 peach halves on the ice cream. (If the peaches are fresh they should be prepared in the following way: boil 2¼ cups water with ¾ cup sugar and simmer the peaches in this syrup for not more than 5 minutes.) Add 2 scoops of ice cream and pour over the purée.

Pears in white wine

3 large pears
½ cup sugar
about ⅔ cup white wine
about ⅔ cup water
strip of lemon peel
2 whole cloves

1   Peel the pears, cut them in half and remove the cores.

2   Place the pears in a saucepan with the remaining ingredients (reserving half the wine) over moderate heat.

3   Simmer until the pears are tender.

4   Drain the pears and place on a serving dish.

5   Add the remaining wine to the cooking liquid. Bring to a boil, lower the heat and simmer for 5–10 minutes.

6   Remove the cloves and lemon peel. Pour the syrup over the pears and allow to cool before serving.

Kiwi bavarois

Preparation: 1 hour
30 minutes

2¾ cups sugar
5 kiwi fruit
1 lemon
2⅓ cups heavy cream
½ stick vanilla
4 egg yolks
2 level tbsp gelatin
2 tbsp apricot jelly
⅓ cup grated coconut

1   Make a syrup by boiling 4½ cups water and 2½ cups sugar. Peel the kiwi fruit; cut them in half, sprinkle with the lemon juice, then leave to stand in the hot syrup for 10 minutes.

2   Gently heat 1½ cups cream with the vanilla; heat 4½ tbsp sugar in a small saucepan until it caramelizes. Pour the caramel into the warm cream and stir. Sift, return to the heat and bring to a boil. Remove from the heat.

3   Beat the egg yolks with 4½ tbsp sugar until creamy. Gradually stir in the caramel cream mixture. Prepare the gelatin according to the manufacturer's instructions and stir into the cream mixture, stirring over very low heat until it thickens and the gelatin is dissolved. Leave to cool. Whip the remaining cream and fold in to the cooled bavarois.

4   Line a mold with foil. Cut the kiwi fruit into rings and place in the bottom.

5   Cover with the bavarois and chill for a few hours. Unmold and brush the top with warmed apricot jelly. Sprinkle with grated coconut.

Chestnut tart

2¼ lb chestnut flour
⅔ cup vegetable oil
1 tbsp sugar
½ tsp salt
¼ cup pine nuts
¼ cup raisins
1 cup or more water
1 sprig rosemary

Chestnut tart or *castagnaccio* is an Italian specialty, from the rural part of northern Tuscany. It can be served hot or cold, though its subtle flavor is more fully appreciated when it is eaten hot.

1   In a large bowl mix together the chestnut flour, oil, sugar, salt, three quarters of the pine nuts and three quarters of the raisins. Add enough water to make a soft batter of pouring consistency.

2   Pour the mixture into a large, low-sided pan which has been brushed with oil: the paste should not be more than ¾–1 in thick.

3   Brush the surface with oil. Sprinkle with the remaining pine nuts, raisins and the rosemary.

4   Cook in a preheated oven at 400°F for 1 hour.

5   Before serving transfer to a serving dish.

Quick apple cake

6 cooking apples
juice of ½ lemon
¼ cup sugar

For the dough:
¼ cup butter or margarine
½ cup sugar
2 egg yolks
juice of ½ lemon
grated peel of ½ lemon
½ cup all-purpose flour
1 tsp baking powder
6 tbsp milk
3 tbsp rum
3 egg whites

For the glaze:
2 tbsp butter or margarine,
   melted
1 egg yolk

1 Peel the apples and
use an apple corer or a
sharp knife to remove the
cores.

2 Sprinkle the apples
with lemon juice and
sugar and put to one side.

3 Cream the butter and
sugar. Beat in the egg
yolks, the juice of half a
lemon and the grated
lemon peel.

4 Sift the flour and
baking powder together
and add to the mixture
together with the milk and
rum.

5 Whisk the egg whites
and fold them carefully
into the mixture, stirring
from bottom to top.

6 Pour the mixture into a
buttered cake tin or
ovenproof pan. Press the
apples into the mixture.
Brush the cake generously
with melted butter and
beaten egg yolk.

7 Bake in a preheated
oven at 325°F for 35–40
minutes.

8 Remove from the
oven and sprinkle with
confectioner's sugar if
liked.

Fruit soufflé omelet

Preparation: 40 minutes

4 eggs, separated
⅓ cup vanilla sugar
2 tbsp flour
1 tbsp lemon juice
salt
2 tbsp butter
1½ cups raspberries
confectioner's sugar
2–3 tbsp rum

1   Beat the egg yolks and vanilla sugar until pale and creamy. Sift the flour and gradually stir into the beaten eggs.

2   Whisk the egg whites with the lemon juice and a pinch of salt until stiff. Fold into the egg yolks using a metal spoon.

3   Heat the butter in a nonstick baking pan and pour in the soufflé omelet mixture. Heat gently for 5–6 minutes until the bottom is golden brown. Transfer to a hot oven (475°F) for 3 minutes. Pour the raspberries into the center and leave in the oven for 1 minute.

4   Slide the omelet on to a serving dish and fold in half. Sprinkle with confectioner's sugar.

5   Heat the rum in a small saucepan; pour over the omelet and flame. Serve at once.

Papaya cups

Preparation: 20 minutes

2 small papaya
3 kiwi fruit
½ cup rum
⅔ cup whipping cream
2 tbsp confectioner's sugar

1   Cut the papaya lengthwise in half and scoop out and discard the black seeds in the middle. Spoon out the flesh and cut into medium-size pieces. Put the empty skins in the freezer.

2   Peel the kiwi fruit and chop. Place all the fruit in a bowl, sprinkle with rum and leave to stand for 1 hour.

3   Just before serving, whip the cream with the confectioner's sugar and spoon into a pastry bag.

4   Spoon the fruit with a little of the juice into the reserved papaya skins; decorate with the whipped cream.

Summer fruit jelly

Preparation: 30 minutes
(+ chilling time)

4 cups (1¼ lb) mixed
   summer fruit
   (strawberries,
   raspberries, bilberries,
   blackberries,
   redcurrants)
1 cup sugar
2½ level tbsp gelatin
2 tbsp kirsch
juice of 1 lemon

1   Place one third of the fruit with the sugar in a saucepan and simmer over low heat for 10 minutes. Strain, then pour the syrup into a saucepan.

2   Prepare the gelatin according to the manufacturer's instructions, then add to the syrup. Stir over low heat until the gelatin is dissolved. Turn off the heat and immediately stir in the kirsch and lemon juice.

3   Rinse four individual molds in water, then pour a little syrup into the bottom of each. Divide the remaining fruit between the molds. Cover with the syrup and refrigerate for several hours.

4   Dip briefly into hot water to unmold.

Tropical jelly mold

Preparation: 30 minutes
(+ chilling time)

2½ cups orange juice
2 level tbsp gelatin
1 1-lb mango
7 oz pineapple slices
7 oz canned lychees
¾ cup whipping cream
2 tbsp confectioner's sugar
grated peel of 2 oranges

1   Sift the orange juice. Prepare the gelatin according to the manufacturer's instructions, dissolving it in 3 tbsp orange juice, then adding the remaining orange juice once it has dissolved.

2   Rinse a 10-inch ring mold in cold water and pour in a layer of gelatin. Place in the freezer.

3   Place the remaining gelatin in the refrigerator. Chop the mango and pineapple and quarter the lychees.

4   As soon as the gelatin begins to set, stir in the fruit and pour into the mold. Refrigerate for at least 3 hours.

5   Whip the cream with the confectioner's sugar, and add the orange peel.

6   Dip the mold briefly in hot water, then turn out. Decorate with the whipped cream.

Desserts and Cakes

Snow cake

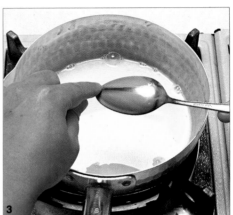

1 sponge cake*
brandy
1 cup milk
¼ cup sugar
2 egg yolks
juice and grated peel of 1
   orange
2 tbsp Curaçao
4 tbsp Grand Marnier
Chantilly cream*

1   Heat the milk and
sugar gently to dissolve
the sugar but do not allow
to boil. Leave to cool
slightly.

2   Beat the egg yolks.
Add the milk and sugar
from step 1.

3   Return this mixture to
the saucepan and stir
constantly. Remove from
the heat just before boiling
point is reached. The
custard should have
thickened sufficiently to
coat the back of a spoon.

4   Add the orange juice
and grated peel, the
Curaçao and 2 tbsp of
Grand Marnier.

5   Cut the sponge into
three layers. Sprinkle with
the remaining Grand
Marnier. Sandwich the
layers with the custard
filling.

6   Pipe the Chantilly
cream flavored with
brandy on the top of the
cake.

Coffee cream cake

For the sponge:
¾ cup sugar
6 eggs, separated
1½ cups all-purpose flour
few drops vanilla extract
coffee liqueur
butter to grease and flour
  to dust pan

*For the coffee butter-
  cream:*
¾ cup + 2 tbsp butter
1½ cups confectioner's
  sugar
2 egg yolks
3 tbsp strong black coffee
few drops vanilla extract

For decoration:
½ cup toasted sliced
  almonds
1 tbsp cocoa powder

1 Beat together the sugar and egg yolks, standing the bowl over a bowl of hot water.

2 Whip the egg whites until stiff and fold gently into the sugar and egg yolk mixture.

3 Sift the flour and fold with the vanilla extract into the mixture.

4 Butter an 8-inch springform pan and dust with flour. Pour the mixture into the pan. Place in a preheated oven at 325°F for 40 minutes.

5 For the buttercream make a sugar syrup with the confectioner's sugar and a little water, allow it to cool, then add it to the egg yolks.

6 Cream the butter and stir in the mixture from step 5. Add the coffee, and mix again.

7 Cut the sponge into three equal layers. Using a pastry brush, brush the layers with coffee liqueur. Spread each layer with coffee buttercream, then cover the entire cake with the remaining cream.

8 Press toasted sliced almonds around the sides of the cake. Decorate the top with cocoa powder: place strips of paper diagonally across the cake in a lattice pattern, as illustrated; sift the cocoa powder over the surface and remove the paper strips.

Sachertorte

5 oz semisweet chocolate
2 tbsp milk
6 eggs, separated
1¼ cups sugar
¾ cup ground almonds
1 cup flour
few drops vanilla extract
1 cup fine breadcrumbs
3–4 tbsp apricot jam
¼ cup rum
chocolate icing*
butter to grease cake pan

1   Melt the chocolate over a low heat with 2 tbsp milk. Whisk the egg whites until stiff.

2   Cream the sugar with the butter, add the egg yolks, melted chocolate, almonds, whisked egg whites, flour, vanilla extract, and breadcrumbs.

3   Pour the mixture into a buttered cake pan and place in a preheated oven at 400°F for 30 minutes. Remove and cool for several hours.

4   Cut the cake into three equal layers. Spread the first with apricot jam. Sprinkle the second layer with rum and place on top. Spread with apricot jam and cover with the third layer.

5   Cover the cake with chocolate icing. Leave smooth, or decorate with more finely piped icing.

Strawberry cream gâteau

1 sponge cake*
Grand Marnier or
    Maraschino to soak
14 oz strawberries
Chantilly cream*

1 Prepare the sponge.

2 When the cake has
cooled cut it into three
equal layers. Sprinkle
each layer with the liqueur
of your choice. Cut 1 cup
strawberries in half.

3 Spread the first layer of
sponge with Chantilly
cream*; cover with
halved strawberries.

4 Repeat with the
second layer.

5 Cover with the third
layer.

6 Cover the entire cake
with Chantilly cream and
decorate with cream
rosettes, using a bag.
Decorate the top and sides
with the remaining
strawberries.

Fruit cake

¼ cup butter
¾ cup confectioner's
  sugar
½ tbsp clear honey
2 eggs
¾ cup flour
1 tsp baking powder
1 cup raisins
1 tbsp walnuts, coarsely
  chopped

2–3 tbsp rum
pinch cinnamon
pinch nutmeg
pinch allspice
2 tbsp chopped candied
  peel
few glacé cherries
butter to grease pan

The fruit cake was an English invention and is justly famous all over the world. The basic recipe can be adapted to give a range of variations: chopped almonds and pistachios can be added, or filberts, or Brazil nuts. Ginger cake is another variation of the same recipe which differs from the other versions in that it contains no nuts or fruit, but is flavored with ginger.

1 Cream the butter until light and smooth.

2 Stir in half the sugar a little at a time.

3 Stir in remaining sugar then add the honey.

4 Add the beaten eggs and mix well using a balloon whisk or electric beater.

5 Sift the flour with the baking powder and add to the mixture. Allow to rest.

6 Soak the raisins and walnuts for about 30 minutes in a mixture of the rum, brandy, cinnamon, nutmeg and allspice. Stir these ingredients together with the candied peel and glacé cherries into the mixture from step 5.

7 Line a rectangular loaf pan with wax paper buttered on both sides. Pour the mixture into the tin and smooth the surface with a spatula.

8 Bake in a preheated oven at 350°F for 1 hour or until cooked. The cake is cooked when a skewer inserted into the middle comes out clean.

Viennese ring

(Kugelhupf)

¼ cup milk
1 cup all-purpose flour
1 whole egg
1¼-oz pkg. active dry
    yeast (1 tbsp)
¼ cup finely chopped
    candied fruit
⅓ cup golden raisins
1 tsp grated lemon peel
½ cup butter
3 egg yolks
almonds or filberts,
    chopped
1 egg and 1 tsp
    confectioner's sugar
butter to grease mold

1   In a basin over simmering water work together the milk, flour, whole egg, yeast and chopped candied peel. Mix in the raisins and grated lemon peel. Allow to rest over the hot water.

2   In a separate bowl mix the butter, confectioner's sugar and egg yolks.

3   Combine the two mixtures.

4   Cover with a cloth and leave to rise over hot water. The dough should double in size.

5   Butter a kugelhupf mold (this has a central tube and high, fluted sides and can be used for savarins and other desserts). Press the chopped nuts to the sides of the tin. Place the dough in the tin and allow to stand for 30 minutes.

6   Bake in a preheated oven at 350°F for about 1 hour. Unmold while still hot and brush with the egg beaten with a little icing sugar. Before serving sprinkle with confectioner's sugar.

Cream puffs

1⅛ cup water
½ cup butter
1 tbsp sugar
½ tsp salt
1¼ cups all-purpose flour
few drops vanilla extract
    or 1 tsp grated lemon
    peel
3–4 eggs
butter to grease and flour
    to dust baking sheet
Chantilly cream* or
    pastry cream*

Choux pastry is used for making profiteroles and chocolate eclairs; it can also be used for savory dishes (with salt, spices or cheese added to the pastry instead of sugar). The filling can be mixed with chopped fresh or candied fruit.

1   Put the water, butter, sugar and salt in a saucepan with high sides and bring to a boil over moderate heat. Turn off the heat as soon as boiling point is reached.

2   Sift the flour into this mixture.

3   Over moderate heat stir vigorously with a wooden spoon until the mixture thickens and begins to sizzle. Remove from the heat and allow to cool, stirring continuously.

4   Add the vanilla extract or the grated lemon peel. Add the eggs one by one, beating each egg a little first and adding it to the mixture gradually.

5   The paste should not be too soft; if it is, it means that the liquid was not reduced enough in step 3. To avoid too soft a mixture add the eggs one at a time, and do not add the fourth egg unless necessary.

6   Butter a baking sheet and dust with flour.

7   Place the paste in little heaps on the baking sheet, using a pastry bag or a spoon. Bake in a preheated oven at 400°F for about 20 minutes. Allow to cool.

8   Prepare the Chantilly cream or the pastry cream and use a pastry bag to fill the puffs with cream. Decorate with more cream, if desired.

Jam drops

½ cup + 2 tbsp butter
½ cup + 3 tbsp sugar
2 eggs
1 tsp grated lemon peel
2 tbsp Marsala
1¾ cups all-purpose flour
¼ cup apricot jam

1   Cream the butter in a bowl and stir in the sugar gradually. Add the eggs, lemon peel and Marsala and mix well. Sift the flour in gradually through a sieve, stirring until well blended. (If the dough is too firm add a few more teaspoons of Marsala.)

2   Allow to stand for an hour or two.

3   Use your hands to shape the dough into small balls about the size of walnuts. Place the dough balls on a buttered cookie sheet and flatten each one with the base of a glass to make "drops" 1¼ in in diameter. Make a well in the center of each one with your finger and fill with 1 tsp jam.

4   Bake in a preheated oven at 350°F for 15 minutes.

Ladyfingers

½ cup + 3 tbsp sugar
6 egg yolks
1¼ cups all-purpose flour
1 tsp salt
6 egg whites
¼ cup confectioner's
    sugar
¼ cup granulated sugar

1   Beat the sugar and egg yolks until creamy. Continuing to beat, gradually add the flour and salt.

2   Whisk the egg whites until they form stiff peaks. Fold carefully into the mixture, stirring from bottom to top until well mixed.

3   Using a pastry bag with a wide plain tube pipe the dough into strips 4 in long on a well-buttered and floured baking tray.

4   Mix the two kinds of sugar and sprinkle over the fingers.

5   Bake in a preheated oven at 325°F for 15–20 minutes.

Brioche croissants

½ oz fresh yeast
¼ cup milk
2¾ cups all-purpose flour
3 tbsp sugar
1 tsp salt
1 whole egg
1 egg yolk
6 tbsp–⅔ cup milk
¼ cup butter
¼–½ cup softened butter
1 egg, beaten with 1 tbsp
   confectioner's sugar
butter to grease and flour
   to dust

1   Mix the yeast with the milk and a few spoonfuls of flour.

2   Make a well in the center of the remaining flour and mix in the sugar, salt, whole egg and yolk, milk and ¼ cup butter.

3   Add the yeast mixture from step 1 and mix thoroughly.

4   Cover and leave to rise in a warm place until doubled in volume.

5   Roll out the dough with a rolling pin.

6   Spread the softened butter over a third of the dough with a spatula.

7   Fold the dough in three and roll out again. Place in the refrigerator for 15 minutes. Fold in three again and roll out with the rolling pin. Leave to rest in the refrigerator for another 15 minutes.

8   Roll out the dough to about ¾ in thick and cut into triangles. Starting from the base roll up each triangle and curve into a crescent shape. Place on a buttered, floured baking sheet and brush with egg beaten with a little icing sugar. Bake in a preheated oven at 450°F for 20 minutes.

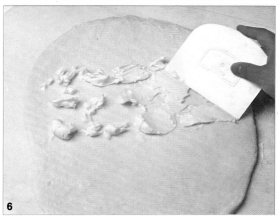

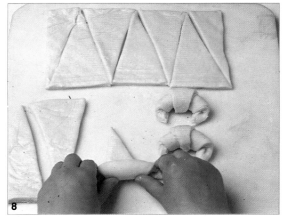

Rum babas

brioche dough*
butter to grease and flour
    to dust molds

For the syrup:
1 cup water
½ cup clear honey
½ cup rum

1   Prepare the dough using the same ingredients and quantities as for the brioches described opposite, but bake the dough in baba molds.

2   To make the syrup: boil the water and honey together for a few minutes. Add the rum and boil for a few minutes more.

3   Soak the warm babas in the rum syrup either by pouring the syrup over them or immersing them in the syrup. Make small holes all over the babas with a skewer to allow the syrup to penetrate. Serve immediately.

Cream doughnuts

3½ cups all-purpose flour
1–2 cups milk
¾ oz fresh yeast
¼ cup + 2 tbsp butter
3 eggs
2–3 tbsp rum
6 tbsp sugar
½ tsp salt
few drops vanilla extract
Pastry cream*
confectioner's sugar

1   Mix ½ cup flour with a little milk and the yeast. Roll the mixture into a ball and set it to rise in warm water until it floats and has doubled in size.

2   Melt the butter; add the eggs and rum. Stir in the remaining flour, sugar, salt and vanilla extract.

3   Add to the ball of yeast and mix well. If necessary add a little milk to make a soft, smooth dough. Set to rise until doubled in volume.

4   Knead the dough on a floured surface for about 15 minutes, until it no longer sticks to the fingers. Roll out to a thickness of ¼–½ in. Using a large glass cut circles from the pastry. Sprinkle with flour and leave in a warm place to rise.

5   Deep fry in plenty of hot oil over moderate heat until golden brown.

6   Drain and fill with pastry cream.

7   Sprinkle with icing sugar.

Scones

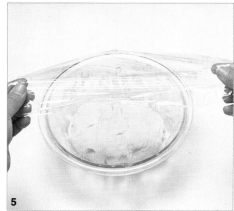

5 cups all-purpose flour
1 tsp baking powder
½ tsp salt
1 tbsp grated orange or
    lemon peel
¼ cup + 2 tbsp butter
6 tbsp sugar
2 eggs
1¼ cups milk or light
    cream
1 beaten egg to glaze

1 Sift the flour together
with the baking powder
and salt into a bowl; add
the grated orange peel.

2 Work in the softened
butter.

3 Add the sugar and mix
until well blended.

4 Add one egg and the
milk or cream and knead
lightly to make a soft
dough.

5 Place the dough in a
bowl and allow to rest for
about 1 hour.

6 Roll out the dough to a
thickness of about ¾ in.
Cut out the scones with a
round pastry cutter.
Transfer to a buttered
baking sheet. Brush the
surface of the scones with
the remaining beaten egg.

7 Bake in a preheated
oven at 400°F for 10–12
minutes.

Madeleines

melted butter to grease
¼ cup + 2 tbsp butter
½ cup confectioner's
   sugar
2 egg yolks
2 tbsp brandy
2 egg whites
½ cup all-purpose flour
pinch salt
¼ cup cornstarch
few drops vanilla essence

This is a classic French recipe from Alsace. The traditional molds are shell shaped. Smaller molds are often used, the resulting biscuits being called *madeleinettes*. When cooled, madeleines or madeleinettes can be dusted with confectioner's sugar.

1   Brush the madeleine molds with a little melted butter.

2   Melt ¼ cup + 2 tbsp butter over hot water.

3   Sift the sugar to eliminate lumps.

4   In a bowl over simmering water mix together the sugar, egg yolks, and brandy and stir until thick. Remove from the heat and transfer the mixture to another bowl to cool.

5   Beat the egg whites and blend in the flour and salt. Fold in mixture from step 4.

6   Add the cornstarch and vanilla essence and mix well.

7   Add the melted butter from step 2 and mix well.

8   Pour the dough into the buttered molds. Bake in a preheated oven at 400°F for about 10 minutes. Remove from the molds at once and cool on a wire rack.

Meringues

3 egg whites
¾ cup granulated sugar

Meringue generally refers to a sweet made with stiffly beaten egg whites and sugar, cooked in a slow oven until firm. The basic recipe—¼ cup sugar to each egg white—can be used to make various shapes, including rings, pyramids, pie crusts and nests. Meringue may also serve as a flan base and can be filled with whipped cream, ice cream, custard or fruit. Flavor and color are affected by flavoring added, such as chocolate, coffee and vanilla. Flat meringues arranged in layers with sponge cake, buttercream, fruit and whipped cream, make an elegant and delicious party dessert.

1   Whisk the egg whites as stiffly as possible using a balloon whisk or electric beater.

2   Sift the sugar and fold in carefully so that the whites do not collapse.

3   Place the mixture in small heaps on a greased baking sheet, using either a spoon or a pastry bag with a large plain tube.

4   Bake immediately in a preheated oven at 225°F until firm and dry.

Zuccotto

4½ cups heavy cream
1 cup confectioner's sugar
1 cup ground almonds
1 cup ground filberts
2–3 tbsp candied fruit
5 oz semisweet chocolate, grated
1 lb sponge cake*
3 tbsp brandy
3 tbsp rum
3 tbsp kirsch
1 tbsp Morello cherries
cocoa powder and confectioner's sugar

1 In a deep bowl whip the cream and fold in the sugar carefully. Add the ground almonds and filberts and candied fruit. Divide the mixture between two bowls. Melt the chocolate, allow it to cool, then fold it into half the cream mixture.

2 Cut the sponge into slices ½–¾ in thick and sprinkle with the three spirits mixed together. Line a mold or bowl with the slices.

3 Pour the plain cream mixture into the mold first. Place the Morello cherries in the center. Pour the chocolate-flavored cream into the mold.

4 Cover the cream with more sponge slices, not dipped in spirit.

5 Chill in the refrigerator for at least 2 hours.

6 Unmold the zuccotto on a serving dish. Decorate with cocoa powder and icing sugar.

Trifle with nuts

1 layer sponge cake*,
   about 1 inch thick
sweet liqueur to soak
confectioner's custard*
Chantilly cream*
toasted nuts or
   caramelized dried fruit*

1   Place the sponge in a glass dish approximately 9 in in diameter.

2   Using a pastry brush, brush the sponge with sweet liqueur of your choice.

3   Spread the sponge with a layer of confectioner's custard ½ in thick.

4   Decorate the cake with toasted nuts or caramelized dried fruit.

5   Place the cake in the freezer for at least 30 minutes.

6   Before serving, decorate the top of the cake with Chantilly cream.

Trifle with meringue topping

2½ cups confectioner's
   custard*
10 oz sponge cake*
few drops red food
   coloring mixed with ¼
   cup liqueur of choice
1 cup candied fruit, diced
¼ cup rum to soak sponge
5 egg whites
1¼ cups icing sugar
candied cherries

1   Place 5 tbsp of the
confectioner's custard in a
large, ovenproof glass dish
and place on top half the
sponge, cut into large
squares and sprinkle with
the liqueur mixture. Cover
with another layer of
custard and four fifths of
the candied fruit.

2   Cover with a second
layer of sponge, sprinkled
with rum, and the
remaining custard.

3   Prepare the meringue
topping by whipping the
egg whites and carefully
folding in the icing sugar.
Cover the sponge with the
meringue and decorate
with the remaining
candied fruit, and candied
cherries.

4   Place in a moderate
oven (350°F) for 3–5
minutes to brown the
meringue.

5   Serve well chilled.

Chocolate mousse

4 egg yolks
½ cup sugar
juice of 1 orange
4 oz semisweet chocolate
¼ cup butter
2 tbsp Marsala or strong
  coffee
1 oz candied orange peel
  (optional)
3 egg whites
1 cup whipping cream,
  lightly whipped

Chocolate mousse differs from all other types of mousse in that it does not contain the classic ingredients of a mousse—gelatin, cornstarch or milk. When chocolate is melted and allowed to cool, it sets the mousse. No other setting agent is needed.

1   In a saucepan beat together the egg yolks and the sugar.

2   Place over low heat, add the orange juice and stir until thickened.

3   Melt the chocolate with the butter and the Marsala or coffee in a bain marie.

4   Stir the chocolate into the egg and orange mixture.

5   Add the candied orange peel.

6   Whisk the egg whites until firm.

7   Fold carefully into the chocolate until the mixture is well blended.

8   Pour into individual dishes or glasses and decorate with a layer of double or whipped cream. Place in the refrigerator until ready to serve.

Cherry liqueur bombe

Preparation: 30 minutes
(+ freezing time)

1 cup sugar
¼ cup maraschino
3 egg yolks
2 cups bottled cherries
⅔ cup heavy cream

1   Mix together in a saucepan ½ cup sugar and the maraschino (reserving 1 tbsp); heat gently, stirring until bubbles form on the surface of the syrup. Remove from the heat and leave to cool.

2   Beat the egg yolks and 3 tbsp sugar in a saucepan until creamy; place in a *bain marie** over low heat and whisk, gradually adding the liqueur syrup in a thin trickle. When frothy and warm, remove from the heat and leave to cool, stirring frequently.

3   Pour the cream into an ice-cream making machine and partially freeze.

4   Add one third of the finely chopped cherries to the cream and finish the freezing process. Divide between four individual molds and place in the freezer for about 1 hour.

5   Meanwhile, blend the remaining fruit, reserving 4 cherries, with the heavy cream, a little sugar and 1 tbsp maraschino. Chill in the refrigerator.

6   Unmold the individual fruit ice creams and pour the chilled cream on top. Decorate with the reserved cherries.

Ice cream

(Vanilla and coffee)

1 cup milk
⅔ cup heavy cream
few drops vanilla extract
3 egg yolks
½ cup icing sugar
1 tbsp coffee powder

1   For the vanilla ice cream boil the milk; for the coffee ice cream boil the milk and coffee. All the other stages and ingredients are the same for both ice creams.

2   Remove from the heat, cool slightly, add the cream and vanilla essence and cool for at least 15 minutes.

3   In a separate bowl beat together the egg yolks and sugar until pale and creamy.

4   Combine the egg yolks and sugar with the mixture from step 2, stirring constantly.

5   Place over a very low heat. Do not boil. Stir constantly until thick.

6   Remove from the heat, transfer to a clean bowl and stir until cool.

7   Pour into a shallow dish and keep in the freezer.

Mint sherbet, orange sherbet

For the mint sherbet:
½ cup sugar
½ cup water
3 tbsp lemon juice
3 tbsp mint syrup
2 egg whites

For the orange sherbet:
½ cup sugar
1¼ cups orange juice
2 tbsp kirsch or
　maraschino
2 egg whites

1　For the mint sherbet (steps 1–6): dissolve the sugar in the water over low heat. Stir until boiling point is reached then remove from the heat.

2　Add the lemon juice and the mint syrup and stir.

3　Whisk the egg whites until stiff and fold into the mixture.

4　Place in a shallow container and freeze for 2 hours.

5　Remove and stir vigorously at intervals to avoid crystals forming as the sherbet freezes.

6　Replace in the freezer to harden and leave until ready to serve.

7　For the orange sherbet: dissolve the sugar in the orange juice over low heat, stirring until thick. Remove from the heat and add the liqueur. Whisk the egg whites and fold in carefully. Place in a container in the freezer for 2 hours. Remove at intervals and beat until smooth. Replace in the freezer until ready to serve.

Yogurt gelatin

6 tsp confectioner's sugar
⅔ cup yogurt
2 tbsp sweet liqueur
⅓ cup heavy cream
1 (¼ oz) envelope
    unflavored gelatin
¼ cup water

1   Mix the sugar and the yogurt. Add the liqueur and stir.

2   Whip the cream until stiff, then fold the cream carefully into the yogurt.

3   Dissolve the gelatin in the hot water and add gradually to the yogurt mixture.

4   Pour into molds, and place in the refrigerator.

5   Turn out into individual glass dishes.

6   Decorate with slices of lime and fresh mint leaves.

Cointreau jellies with orange sauce

1 (¼ oz) envelope
   unflavored gelatin
¼ cup hot water
¼ cup sugar
2 egg yolks
1¼ cups milk
3 tbsp Cointreau
2 egg whites

1 Put the gelatin and the hot water in a bowl to soften the gelatin.

2 Beat together the sugar and egg yolks until creamy. Add the milk and mix.

3 Add the gelatin and the liqueur.

4 Keep the mixture warm over a bowl of hot water until needed.

5 Beat the egg whites until stiff.

6 Fold carefully into the cream, stirring carefully from bottom to top.

7 Pour into molds and allow to set.

8 Prepare the orange sauce. To make the orange sauce, dissolve the sugar in the orange juice over low heat. Bring to a boil, then remove from the heat. Allow to cool. To serve, turn out the individual molds on to a serving dish and pour round the orange sauce.

Basic Recipes

The following section lists, in alphabetical order, ingredients, utensils, and preparation instructions referred to in the book.

AÏOLI

4 cloves garlic
2 egg yolks
salt and pepper
1⅛ cups olive oil
1 lemon

Peel the garlic and crush in a mortar. Stir together the egg yolks, garlic, and salt and pepper. Pour in the oil a drop at a time, stirring constantly. Add the lemon juice in the same way and continue stirring until smooth.

ALMOND PASTE

1 lb almonds
2¼ cups granulated sugar
¼ cup white corn syrup
¾ cup water
confectioner's sugar, if needed

Preheat oven to 350°F. Soak almonds in boiling water 5 to 10 minutes or until skins loosen and can be peeled off easily. Peel almonds; place on a baking sheet. Place in oven to dry and toast. Toast only until lightly colored, about 5 minutes. If allowed to burn, almonds cannot be used for almond paste. Grind toasted almonds in batches in a blender or food processor to make a fine flour. Lightly oil a marble slab or baking sheet. In a medium saucepan, dissolve granulated sugar and corn syrup in water. Boil until mixture reaches the soft-ball stage (238°F). While still hot, blend sugar syrup with ground almonds. Pour mixture onto oiled marble or baking sheet. Work with a spatula until mixture is cool enough to handle. Then knead until smooth, dusting with powdered sugar as needed. For immediate use, let paste stand at least 2 hours. Store tightly covered in a cool place. If paste becomes too hard to shape easily, wrap in foil and steam over boiling water until softened. Almond paste can be colored or flavored with liqueurs or extracts. Makes about 2 lb.

BAIN MARIE & DOUBLE BOILER

The term *bain marie* describes a method of cooking liquid or solid foods in a container placed in boiling water. To make a *bain marie*, place a saucepan or small baking pan, soufflé dish or ramekins in a baking pan half-full of water. The outer pan should be no more than half-full so no water splashes into the food.

A double boiler is two pans fitted one inside the other. The bottom pan holds water that does not touch the top pan.

Both methods are generally used for cooking sauces, custards and egg dishes, and when melting chocolate. It prevents them from overheating or curdling and keeps them hot. The temperature of the food never reaches the boiling point.

BAKING

Oven temperatures are as follows:

Cool	250 to 300°F
Warm	300 to 325°F
Moderate	325 to 400°F
Hot	400 to 450°F

Always preheat the oven before baking cakes, cookies, soufflés, sweet breads and other desserts unless the recipe dictates otherwise. Plan your recipe preparation and preheating of the oven so food doesn't have to wait for the oven to heat.

During baking, keep the oven door closed. Opening the door will cause the temperature to drop. Cakes and soufflés, in particular, might be ruined. If it is absolutely unavoidable or if the recipe instructs you to do so, carefully open the door, avoiding a sudden draft of air. Close it as quickly as possible.

BÉARNAISE SAUCE

Makes approximately 1⅛ cups
2 shallots
½ cup white wine
4 tbsp vinegar
1½ tbsp chopped tarragon
1½ tbsp chopped chervil
3 egg yolks
1 cup + 2 tbsp butter
salt
pinch Cayenne pepper

Finely chop the shallots and place in a saucepan with the wine, vinegar, and 1 tablespoon each tarragon and chervil. Reduce over low heat for about 15 minutes until approximately 4 tablespoons of liquid remain. Strain through a chinois, pressing well to extract as much liquid as possible. Pour into a double saucepan or into a small basin over a saucepan of simmering water. Mix in the egg yolks, beating with a whisk. Gradually add the softened butter, beating carefully and making sure that each piece is well blended before adding the next. Remove from the heat and continue beating. The sauce should be quite thick. Add the remaining tarragon and chervil and season with salt and Cayenne pepper. Mix well.

BEEF CONSOMMÉ

2½ pints homemade meat stock, all fat removed
½ lb stewing beef
1 onion
1 clove garlic
1 carrot
1 celery stalk
pinch of thyme
3 peppercorns
1 egg white
salt

Trim off any fat from the beef; mince or chop finely and place in a large pot or saucepan. Scrub the carrot, peel the onion and chop them with the celery and garlic and add to the beef. Add a pinch of salt, the thyme, the egg white and the black peppercorns and mix well. Pour in the cold beef stock and bring to a boil, stirring constantly. Turn down the heat, cover and simmer for 1 hour. Strain the consommé through a fine sieve lined with a piece of muslin before serving.

BEEF CONSOMMÉ WITH SHERRY

Follow the recipe above, stirring in 6 tablespoons medium dry sherry at the end of the cooking time, before straining.

BEURRE BLANC

1 shallot, chopped
2 tbsp white wine vinegar
1½ tbsp white wine
1½ tbsp fumet (*q.v.*)
½ cup butter
salt and pepper

Place the shallot, vinegar, wine, and fumet in a saucepan and cook over moderate heat until the liquid has reduced by three quarters. Remove from the heat. Leave to cool slightly before beating in the butter as quickly as possible, one piece at a time. Make sure the butter is well blended and the sauce pale and creamy. Season with salt and pepper. (If the sauce turns transparent, plunge the bottom of the saucepan into iced water until the sauce thickens.)

BUTTER CREAM

¾ cup + 2 tbsp butter or margarine
1 cup confectioner's sugar
4 egg yolks
2 egg whites, if desired

In a medium bowl, cream butter or margarine and sugar until light and fluffy. Beat in egg yolks, 1 at a time. Whisk egg whites until stiff but not dry. Gently fold beaten egg whites into butter mixture. Makes about 2½ cups.

Variations:

Vanilla butter cream
Beat in 1½ teaspoons vanilla extract with egg yolks.

Liqueur butter cream
Beat in 2 tablespoons liqueur of choice with egg yolks.

Hazelnut butter cream
After folding in beaten egg whites, fold in ½ cup ground toasted hazelnuts.

Pistachio or almond butter cream
After folding in beaten egg whites, fold in ¼ to ½ cup finely chopped or ground pistachios or almonds.

Lemon butter cream
Beat in 2 tablespoons lemon juice with egg yolks.

Chocolate butter cream
Beat in 2 ounces melted unsweetened chocolate with egg yolks.

Coffee butter cream
Beat in 2 teaspoons instant coffee powder with egg yolks.

Pistachio Grand Marnier butter cream
Beat in 2 tablespoons Grand Marnier with egg yolks. After folding in beaten egg whites, fold in ¼ cup finely chopped or ground pistachios.

CAPER SAUCE
2 tbsp capers
1 clove garlic
1 tbsp anchovy paste
1⅛ cups olive oil
juice of ½ lemon

Pound the capers and garlic or blend in a food processor. Place in a bowl and mix in the anchovy paste. Stir in the olive oil gradually, followed by the lemon juice, and mix until well blended.

CARAMELIZED FRUIT
⅔ cup sugar
⅓ cup water
fruit of your choice

In a small saucepan, cook sugar and water until light brown. Dip fruit in caramelized sugar. Allow the sugar to harden, then dip the fruit in caramelized sugar again. Makes about ⅓ cup.

Both fresh and dried fruit can be caramelized by following this method. Candied fruit and citrus peel can also be caramelized. These can be sandwiched together with a marzipan filling (*q.v.*) before being caramelized.

CHANTILLY CREAM
2 cups whipping cream
2–4 tbsp confectioner's sugar

In a large bowl, whip cream until soft peaks form. Beat in sugar to taste until stiff peaks form. Makes about 3½ cups.

Chantilly cream is sweetened whipped cream. Unsweetened whipped cream and whipped cream with sugar and vanilla extract added are sometimes incorrectly called Chantilly cream. In spite of extensive research, no one knows where or when the name originated.

CHICKEN STOCK
bones and carcass of 1 chicken
½ leek
1 onion, halved
2 carrots
1 bouquet garni

12 peppercorns
salt
1 bay leaf

Place all the ingredients in a large saucepan or stockpot. Cover with cold water and bring to a boil. Skim, cover, and simmer for 3 hours. Strain, and allow the stock to cool. When cold, remove the solid white fat, strain again, and store in the refrigerator or freezer.

CHOCOLATE FROSTING
1 cup whipping cream
7 oz semisweet chocolate
½ cup confectioner's sugar
1 tsp vanilla extract

Combine the cream and 5 oz chocolate. Cook over medium heat until chocolate melts and mixture begins to boil. Stir well. Refrigerate until slightly warm. Beat until smooth. Beat in confectioner's sugar and vanilla.

CLARIFIED BUTTER
1 lb butter

Melt the butter in a saucepan over moderate heat and simmer for 5 minutes. Remove any surface scum with a slotted spoon, then pour the clarified butter into a clean basin, making sure the residue which collects in the bottom of the saucepan is left behind.

COCOA & CHOCOLATE
Cocoa powder is extracted from fruit seeds of the cocoa plant grown in tropical regions of the world. Each cocoa fruit is 8 to 10 inches long and contains as many as 60 seeds.

The process of extracting cocoa is complicated. Seeds are allowed to ferment in the open air or underground. Then they are washed, dried, roasted and fermented a second time. They are again washed and dried, then they are ground. At this time, cocoa butter is separated from the seeds. Cocoa seeds contain a large quantity of oil and fat that is used in the manufacture of cosmetics, medicines and chocolate.

The major use of cocoa is for the manufacture of chocolate, but it is widely used in pastries, confections and in milk drinks.

Chocolate is manufactured by heating cocoa powder with a good portion of cocoa butter. It is then allowed to set up in various shapes and thicknesses. To melt chocolate, grate or break block chocolate into small pieces. Place in top of a double boiler or in a saucepan over or in a pan of simmering water. If the melting chocolate remains thick or develops lumps, add a little margarine—never butter—and reduce the heat. Unused chocolate can be saved, but must be melted again.

COOKIES
Cookies are usually sweet and are made with liquid, flour, butter, sugar, eggs and flavorings. They are quite easy to make. Use fresh ingredients, and be sure to measure them carefully. Use baking sheets with very low or no edges. Baking pans with high sides prevent cookies from browning evenly. Bake cookies in the center of the oven if only one baking sheet is being used. If two baking sheets are being used at the same time, leave space between them for air to circulate. Cut cookies the same size to ensure even cooking.

Types of cookies:

Bars
Are baked in one piece, then cut into slices or squares when cooled.

Dropped
Cookies are made with dough that is too soft to be rolled with a rolling pin. The dough is spooned onto the baking sheet.

Rolled
Cookies are flattened with a rolling pin, then cut out with fancy cutters or shaped by hand.

Piped
Means the dough is piped through a pastry bag, according to the shape desired.

Refrigerator dough is usually rolled into a cylinder and stored in the refrigerator or freezer. When firm, it is sliced or shaped into thin cookies.

Some cookies are sandwiched together with cream cheese, jam, flavored creams or fruit fillings. Tops of cookies may be decorated with chocolate or glacé icing, nuts, candied fruit, jam, granulated or confectioner's sugar, coconut or other decorative items.

Cookies keep best in an airtight container or in the freezer wrapped in foil. Never put crisp and soft, moist cookies together in the same container. The moisture from the moist cookies will soften crisp cookies.

CONFECTIONER'S CUSTARD
1 cup + 2 tbsp milk
1 cup + 2 tbsp half and half
1 tsp grated lemon peel or orange peel, or 1 tsp vanilla extract
¾ cup sugar
1 tsp cornstarch
10 egg yolks, beaten

Reserve ⅓ cup milk. In a medium saucepan, combine remaining milk and half and half. Place over low heat. Add lemon or orange peel or vanilla. Gradually add sugar, stirring constantly. Blend reserved ⅓ cup milk with cornstarch. Add to hot milk mixture. Stirring constantly, bring to a boil. Remove from heat. Add 1 cup hot milk mixture slowly to beaten egg yolks. Then add egg-yolk mixture to hot milk mixture, stirring constantly. Return to heat until mixture thickens. Do not overcook. This can be done in a double boiler to prevent overcooking. Makes about 3½ cups.

COURT-BOUILLON

1 carrot
5 peppercorns
9 cups water
½ cup white wine
¼ cup white wine vinegar
½ tbsp sea salt
½ celery stalk
2 sprigs parsley
½ onion
½ bay leaf
pinch thyme

Cut the carrot into four lengthwise, crush the peppercorns, and place all the ingredients in a large saucepan. Bring to a boil, simmer for 30 minutes, then strain through a sieve. This rich *court-bouillon* is ideal for fish such as turbot and eel. For a simpler version, reduce the quantity of vegetables and use half the quantity of wine and vinegar. This quantity will be sufficient for 2¼ lb fish.

CREAM CUSTARD

1½ cups milk
½ cup powdered sugar
1 tbsp all-purpose flour
1 tbsp cornstarch
2 egg yolks, beaten
1 tbsp butter

In a medium saucepan, scald 1 cup milk. In a medium bowl, combine remaining ½ cup milk, sugar, flour and cornstarch; stir to blend. Add mixture to scalded milk. Simmer, stirring constantly, until thickened. Add ½ to ¾ cup hot mixture to beaten egg yolks; then add egg-yolk mixture to remaining milk mixture, stirring constantly. Add butter, beating well. Return to heat until mixture simmers. Cool. Makes about 2 cups.

CREAMED PEPPER SAUCE

2 sweet peppers
⅔ cup light cream
salt

Place the sweet peppers in a hot oven, 400°F, or under the broiler until the skins blister and can be rubbed off. Skin the peppers and discard the seeds. Cut into small pieces and place in a blender or food processor with the cream and a pinch of salt. Blend until smooth; transfer to a small saucepan or skillet, cover and simmer for 5 minutes, stirring with a whisk. Serve with pasta.

DEEP FRYING

When deep frying, use a pan with high sides so the oil will not overflow when food is being cooked.

Recipes often call for moderately hot, hot and very hot fat. These are as follows:

Moderately hot fat
Uses a low, steady heat to cook food inside before the outside becomes too crisp or begins to burn.

Hot fat
Has a constant, moderate heat underneath. It is used for sweets that are already partly cooked then coated in batter. The outside is cooked until crisp and golden without overcooking the inside.

Very hot fat
Uses high heat to cook small pieces of food that must cook rapidly without burning.

After frying one batch of food, let the oil become hot again before adding more food. If the oil is not hot enough, it soaks into the food, making it soggy and preventing a crisp, golden crust.

If you do not have a deep-fat thermometer, use the bread-cube method to determine temperatures. When deep frying, a 1-inch cube of bread will turn golden brown at these temperatures and times:

345–355°F	65 seconds
356–365°F	60 seconds
366–375°F	50 seconds
376–385°F	40 seconds
386–395°F	20 seconds

FISH

Choosing fish

For serious cooks and lovers of fish, truly fresh fish can only be considered that which, as soon as it is caught, is sorted into shallow boxes on a bed of ice and transported immediately to a quayside market. When buying fish it is essential to know how to judge its freshness from its appearance, texture, and smell.

Freshly caught fish is quite stiff, although this characteristic changes after only a few hours; the skin is taut, bright, and shiny; the scales lie flat against the body, which is covered with a thin, translucent film. The pupil should be dark and bright and the cornea shining and transparent. The flesh beneath the gill flap should be bright red and the fish should be firm and resistant to the touch; the flesh should spring back when pressed lightly.

As for judging the freshness of fish by its smell, a few simple comparisons may help: fresh fish should smell of the sea and of the strong but pleasant saltiness of seaweed. When checking the freshness of molluscs and crustaceans the appearance of the body is the most important indicator; crustaceans should be shiny, wet, and firm, vividly colored with their legs or claws firmly attached to their bodies. They should smell fresh and of the sea. The color of the body of molluscs may vary, depending on their color when caught, as they often camouflage themselves. The whiteness of the flesh of cuttlefish and squid is a sign of freshness; yellow or brownish patches show that they are not fresh. The state of the shells is a good indication of the freshness of mussels, clams, or oysters. They should be tightly closed or should snap shut when sharply tapped if the molluscs are still alive. As with fish, they should smell pleasantly salty and fresh.

Cooking fish

Fish lends itself to a variety of cooking methods, depending on the quality and texture of the flesh: it can be poached, cooked in foil (en papillote), shallow-fried, deep fried, baked, grilled or broiled, barbecued, braised, or steamed.

Poaching
The fish is cooked by simmering in a rich vegetable *court-bouillon* (*q.v.*) or lighter stock, depending on the type of fish. The stock should be allowed to cool before use and should always be kept below boiling point while the fish is cooking.

Cooking in foil
Fish cooked *en papillote* is placed together with the herbs and seasonings in the center of a well-buttered sheet of foil. The edges are folded tightly to seal, forming a loose parcel, and the fish is baked in the oven or cooked in a steamer.

Shallow frying
Suitable for fillets and steaks. The fish is usually floured then fried in melted butter or oil.

Deep frying
Suitable for whole fish or fillets coated in batter. The fish is cooked in hot oil (350–370°F) and should be well drained on kitchen paper to absorb excess fat before serving.

Baking
All the ingredients, including the fish, are placed in an ovenproof dish or casserole and baked in the oven.

Broiling or barbecuing
The most important points to remember when cooking fish this way are the evenness of temperature and the distance of the fish from the source of heat. The fish should be slowly and evenly cooked. To prepare the fish, either soak in brine or brush with oil. Brush several times during cooking.

Braising
In this method the fish is browned lightly first in a little melted butter and then cooked either in the oven or on top of the stove in wine, stock, tomato sauce, or other liquid.

Steaming
The fish is cooked, with herbs and seasonings, on a plate or wrapped in foil and placed in a perforated metal basket or steamer over a saucepan of simmering water.

Storing fish
To keep fish for a short period—not more than 24 hours—clean in the usual way, wrap in plastic wrap, and place in the refrigerator. To keep fish for longer than a day it should be stored in the freezer. Rinse and clean the fish thoroughly, dry with kitchen paper, and cut into fillets or steaks. Frozen fish, which—strictly speaking—should have been brought from room temperature to 0°F in less than 4 hours, should be stored at that temperature until it is used. Frozen fish is usually packaged in plastic bags so that you can check the state of the fish. Once removed from the freezer it must be used without delay. Always pay careful attention to the recommended storage dates on frozen fish.

FISH ASPIC
1 onion
1 carrot
1 celery stalk
oil
bouquet garni
¾ lb fish trimmings (heads, bones, etc.)
water
5 oz white filleted fish
1 egg
3 tbsp dry white wine
1 envelope gelatin (optional)

Sauté an onion, a carrot and a celery stalk in a little oil in a large saucepan together with a bouquet garni. When the vegetables have softened, add the fish trimmings and water and bring to a boil. Simmer, covered, for 30 minutes. Remove from the heat and strain through a fine sieve. To clarify the liquid, allow to cool completely and then add the white filleted fish, and the white of an egg and the shell, finely crushed. Beat well with a balloon whisk and heat gently for 10–15 minutes. When the liquid is tepid, add the dry white wine and stir. Strain through a muslin cloth. In order to ensure that the fish aspic sets more rapidly and reliably, you can add an envelope of gelatin, dissolved in the fish aspic over gentle heat.

FISH FUMET
1½ quarts of water
1 cup dry white wine
1½ lb fish trimmings (heads, bones, etc.)
1 onion
1 celery stalk
1 carrot
1 bay leaf
black peppercorns

Bring the water and wine to a boil in a large saucepan. Add the fish trimmings, sliced onion, the celery stalk, carrot, bay leaf and a few black peppercorns. Simmer gently over

moderate heat for 40 minutes; leave to cool and then strain through a fine sieve.

FISH STOCK
½ lb fish trimmings (heads, bones, etc.)
1 lb assorted fish
2 quarts water
1 cup dry white wine
1 celery stalk
1 leek
1 onion
1 bay leaf
pinch of thyme
salt

Coarsely chop the fish trimmings and place in a large saucepan with 1 lb assorted fish. Pour in the water and dry white wine. Bring slowly to boiling point. Add the coarsely chopped celery, the leek, and the peeled and quartered onion, a bay leaf, a pinch of thyme and a little salt. Simmer gently for 40 minutes. Strain.

FRANGIPANE CREAM
2 egg yolks
½ cup sugar
¼ cup all-purpose flour
¼ cup finely ground almonds
2 cups milk
vanilla extract

In a large bowl, beat egg yolks and sugar until pale and creamy. Beat in flour and ground almonds. Gradually stir in milk and vanilla. Place a fine sieve over a medium saucepan. Pour mixture through sieve to remove any lumps. Stir constantly over low heat until thick and smooth. Makes about 3 cups.

GLAZES

Honey glaze
Melt honey over low heat with a few spoonfuls of water.

Honey glaze with liqueur
To the above add a few drops of liqueur. Stir until blended and slightly reduced. The spirit most often used is rum. White rum gives a pale glaze while dark rum results in a dark glaze.

Jam glaze
Melt a few tablespoons of jam over low heat. The jam will become more liquid and will be easy to brush while still warm. For a thinner glaze, dilute jam with a little water. The jams most frequently used in baking are apricot, which gives a golden glaze, and raspberry, which gives a reddish glaze. Fruit jelly can also be used as a glaze in the same way.

Rum glaze
Melt confectioner's sugar with a little rum in a saucepan over low heat. Stir to blend. Use 1 to 2 tablespoons rum per 1 cup confectioner's sugar.

HOLLANDAISE SAUCE
2 large egg yolks
1 tbsp white wine vinegar
salt and pepper
scant 1 cup butter
1 tbsp lemon juice

Beat together in a small basin or double boiler the egg yolks, vinegar, and salt and pepper. Heat very gently over a saucepan of gently simmering water, stirring constantly and adding the butter one piece at a time. Make sure each piece is well blended before adding the next. When all the butter is added and the sauce coats the back of a spoon, remove from the heat and stir in the lemon juice. Mix well and serve hot.

HSAO MAI DUMPLING CASES
2 cups strong flour
pinch salt
Makes 36

Sift the flour into a bowl; form a well in the center and add scant 1 cup boiling water, stirring quickly until a smooth, fairly thick dough is obtained. Knead the dough for 3 minutes and then roll into a long, cylindrical sausage shape.

Cut the roll into 36 portions and roll each portion into a ball. Flour the pastry board lightly and, using a lightly floured rolling pin, roll each ball out into a circle about 2¾ in in diameter.

The dough sheets can be kept in the refrigerator if made in advance.

ICE CREAM, SHERBET & SORBET
Basic ingredients of ice cream are sugar, milk or cream, eggs and flavoring, such as vanilla, chocolate, lemon or strawberry. Ice cream is made by blending the ingredients as they freeze or freezing the blended ingredients, then beating to make them smooth and creamy.

Sherbets are frozen combinations of fruit purées, such as pineapple, orange and strawberry, blended with sugar syrup or another sweetener. Gelatin or whipped egg white are sometimes added to give them a light, fluffy texture.

Sorbet is made from fruit purée, juice and sweeteners or may contain wine or liqueur. It contains no milk or eggs, and must be stirred during freezing to reduce the ice crystals. Or, the frozen mixture can be scraped to resemble finely crushed ice.

ICING
Icing is used to cover cakes, breads and rolls. Use a soft icing on breads and rolls so it can be drizzled. When the icing will be spread, it must be soft enough to spread easily before it hardens. Cake icing should be thick so it does not drip.

A very thin icing can be used as a glaze. Spread it over the cake. Let it dry before adding the thicker icing. This keeps crumbs from mixing with the icing. Fruit-based jellies can also be used as glazes.

Fondant icing
1½ cups sugar
½ teaspoon cream of tartar
¾ cup water

In a large, heavy saucepan, combine sugar and cream of tartar. Stir in water. Stir over low heat until sugar dissolves. Cover and bring to a boil. Remove cover; boil until mixture reaches soft-ball stage (238°F). Cool to room temperature. Beat vigorously with a wooden spoon until white and creamy. Use immediately to ice a cake. If fondant becomes too stiff to spread, add a little hot water, then beat until smooth. Makes about 2 cups.

Glacé icing
2 cups confectioner's sugar
3–5 tbsp hot water

Sieve powdered sugar into a large bowl. Confectioner's sugar should always be sieved before making icing. Stir in water, a little at a time, until mixture forms a thick, smooth paste of coating consistency.

Variations
Add any of the following flavorings: cocoa powder, chocolate, coffee, Grand Marnier or other liqueurs, orange, lemon, caramel, cream cheese, strawberry, cherry, milk, fruit juice, almond extract, rose water or vanilla extract. Icing can also be tinted any desired color.

Weeping icing
Add more water so mixture is thinner. This is often used on babas.

Royal icing
In place of water, use 1 egg white for each 1½ cups confectioner's sugar. Lightly beat egg white. Sift sugar as it is gradually stirred into egg white. Add a few drops of lemon juice to make icing whiter. Icing is ready when it will stand up in peaks. Store in a glass container. To use again, heat gently; add a few drops of water, if necessary.

LEAVENING AGENTS

Yeast
When combined with flour, moisture and warmth, yeast begins to ferment and converts flour into alcohol and carbon dioxide. These gas bubbles are what leavens bread. Oven heat kills the yeast and causes the gas to expand, raising the bread in a final *oven spring*.

Active dry yeast comes in ¼-oz envelopes or in bulk. *Compressed fresh yeast* comes in .06-oz cakes. One envelope of dry yeast equals 1 scant tablespoon dry

yeast or 1 cake compressed fresh yeast.

Active dry yeast has been dehydrated. The cells become active when mixed with a warm liquid. Store dry yeast in a cool, dry place—not in the refrigerator or freezer. Use by the expiration date on the package. Or, *proof the yeast* by combining 1 envelope active dry yeast or 1 cake compressed fresh yeast, 1 teaspoon sugar and ¼ cup warm water. If the yeast begins to bubble and swell, it is active. If not, discard the yeast and begin with another package.

Compressed fresh yeast must be refrigerated and used within 1 to 2 weeks or by the expiration date on the package. It should always be proofed.

Baking soda or bicarbonate of soda
This reacts when moistened. It is especially volatile when combined with an acid liquid, such as buttermilk. It immediately gives off carbon dioxide. Always blend it with other dry ingredients before it is moistened, then bake as soon as possible.

Baking powder
This is a combination of baking soda and cream of tartar. *Single-acting* baking powder immediately releases its gas into the batter. *Double-acting* baking powder releases some gas when it is moistened and again when the batter is heated.

To ensure even distribution of baking soda or baking powder and even rising of the dough, blend with other dry ingredients before adding liquid.

Too much baking soda or baking powder gives a baked product a dry, crumbly texture and a bitter taste. It also causes the product to overrise and fall. Too little baking soda or baking powder makes a product heavy and gummy.

LEMON MARINADE
2–3 lemons

Lemons are used as a marinade for raw fish. Clean, rinse, and dry the fish and leave to stand in the lemon juice for 30 minutes to 1 hour, depending on the size of the fish. Do not leave for too long as the acid will make the flesh flaccid.

MARZIPAN
2¼ cups granulated sugar
⅔ cup water
pinch of cream of tartar
3 cups finely ground, blanched almonds
2 egg whites, beaten stiff but not dry
½ to ¾ cup powdered sugar

Lightly oil a marble slab or baking sheet. Dissolve granulated sugar in water over medium heat. Add cream of tartar; stir until dissolved. Boil without stirring until mixture reaches the soft-ball stage (238°F). Remove from heat. Stir in almonds and beaten egg whites. Return to heat 2 to 3 minutes,

stirring constantly. Turn onto oiled marble or baking sheet. Work paste with a spatula 5 to 10 minutes, bringing edges to center. When cool enough to work by hand, knead until smooth. Use powdered sugar, if necessary, to keep paste from sticking. Makes about 2 pounds.

Marzipan can be used to decorate large cakes or it can be made into small marzipan cakes. It can be shaped and colored in a variety of ways, and is often molded into fruit-shapes that can be glazed and colored.

Marzipan and almond paste (*q.v.*) are similar, and are often confused. Almond paste is used mainly as a filling for cakes and cookies. Marzipan is used mainly for decoration.

MAYONNAISE
2 eggs
salt
¾–1 cup best quality olive oil
juice of ¼ lemon

Separate two eggs and beat the yolks lightly with a fork, seasoning with a little salt. Add to the yolks ¾–1 cup of very good quality olive oil a few drops at a time, beating with a wooden spoon until the mayonnaise thickens. Carefully beat in the juice of quarter of a lemon, adding a few drops at a time. This basic mayonnaise, perhaps the most famous of all cold sauces, can be flavored in many different ways for a wide variety of dishes.

Green mayonnaise
mayonnaise made with 2 egg yolks (see recipe above)
2 oz spinach
a few basil leaves
small bunch parsley
salt and pepper

Wash the spinach leaves thoroughly in cold running water to remove all traces of grit. Cook briefly in a covered saucepan with no added water. Drain when tender and chop finely. Chop the basil and parsley and mix with the spinach. Work into the mayonnaise and season with salt and pepper.

MEAT ASPIC
2 veal shanks
2 calf's feet
3½ oz pork rind
1 onion
1 celery stalk
1 carrot
bouquet garni (parsley, thyme, bay leaf)
salt
2 quarts water
2 eggs

Place all the ingredients, with the exception of the egg whites and shells, in a large saucepan. Bring to a boil over high heat. Turn down the heat and simmer very gently for 2–3 hours, or until the liquid has reduced to half its original volume. Skim off any scum that rises to the top. Strain the stock through a fine sieve. Leave to cool then clarify by adding the whites and crushed shells of two eggs; return to a clean saucepan and heat gently over low heat, stirring with a balloon whisk. When the stock reaches boiling point simmer for 10 minutes. Turn off the heat and leave to cool for 10 minutes before straining through a damp muslin cloth.

MEAT SAUCE

1 tbsp butter
10 oz ground beef
2 oz fresh spicy sausage
1 bay leaf
½ onion
1 clove
salt
8 oz tomatoes

Melt the butter in a heavy saucepan; add the ground beef, crumbled sausage, bay leaf and the ½ onion stuck with a clove, and cook over low heat for 20 minutes, stirring frequently. Add salt and the skinned, seeded and chopped tomatoes; bring to a boil and simmer for about 1 hour, adding a little stock or warm water and 1 tsp meat extract if the sauce becomes too dry. Cook for a further 20 minutes then remove the onion and bay leaf.

MOCK MEAT SAUCE

1 onion
1 celery stalk
1 carrot
1 tbsp olive oil
2 oz fatty ham
1⅛ cups white wine
12 oz tomatoes
salt and pepper
1 tbsp chopped fresh parsley and marjoram

Mince the onion, celery and carrot. Heat the olive oil in a skillet and brown the chopped vegetables and finely sliced ham. Add the wine, heat for 2 minutes then add the chopped tomatoes. Season with salt and pepper and cook over medium heat for about 45 minutes.

MORNAY SAUCE

¼ cup + 3 tbsp butter
¼ cup flour
1⅛ cups milk
salt
½ cup grated Parmesan

Make a white sauce: Melt 3 tbsp butter in a small saucepan, add the flour and stir over heat for 1 minute. Gradually stir in the hot milk, waiting for the sauce to thicken after each addition. Add salt to taste, then simmer for about 10 minutes. Add the remaining butter, cut into pieces, and the grated Parmesan and mix well. This sauce goes very well with fish.

NANTUA SAUCE

8 oz freshwater crayfish
salt
½ cup + 2 tbsp butter
¼ cup flour
1⅛ cup milk
1⅛ cup fumet (q.v.)
pepper
¾ cup heavy cream

Boil the crayfish whole in salted water for 8 minutes without peeling; chop into pieces while still hot. Place in a blender or food processor with ½ cup melted butter and liquidize. Strain through a fine sieve.

Make a white sauce: melt the remaining butter in a saucepan. Stir in the flour and cook gently for 2 minutes. Remove from the heat and stir in a little hot milk. Beat until smooth. Return to the heat and add the remaining milk and fumet. Season with salt and pepper. Bring to a boil, then simmer for 3 minutes. Add the cream and reduce slightly. Remove from the heat and stir in the crayfish butter.

NUTS, GRINDING & TOASTING

Almonds, hazelnuts, and peanuts can all be ground coarsely or to a fine meal—similar to flour—for use in desserts. When a recipe calls for ground almonds, the nuts should be ground fine, like flour. Use a blender or the fine blade of a food grinder to pulverize the nuts. Remove skins before grinding. Some skins will come off when nuts are rubbed between your hands. To remove almond skins, boil 5 minutes in water to cover.

To toast nuts, spread skinless nuts on a baking sheet. Toast in a 350°F oven until browned as desired. Do not let them burn or they will become bitter and unusable. Grind coarsely or finely, as needed for each recipe.

PANCAKES FOR SPRING ROLLS

sifted strong flour
pinch of salt
peanut oil

Mix 2 parts flour with 1 part water and a pinch of salt to make a thick mixture. Leave to stand for 1 hour. Heat a griddle or skillet and brush very lightly with peanut oil.

Take up a handful of the mixture, which should be quite elastic in consistency, and spread out on the griddle, shaping a pancake approx. 6 in diameter. As the mixture cooks (the heat should not be too high) a thin pancake will form which should be carefully peeled off the griddle. Clean the griddle between pancakes with a cloth dipped in oil and repeat the procedure until the required number of pancakes or spring roll skins have been prepared. These spring roll skins can be kept in the refrigerator, covered with a damp cloth.

PANCAKES, MANDARIN (FOR PEKING DUCK)

2 cups strong flour
sesame seed oil

Sift the flour into a large bowl and make a well in the center. Pour scant ⅓ cup boiling water into the well and work into the flour. Add ½ cup cold water a little at a time and blend into the flour using a wooden spoon until the dough is smooth and soft. Work the dough for a further 5 minutes, cover with a damp cloth and leave for 20 minutes.

Roll the dough into a long, cylindrical sausage and cut into 24 pieces. Roll each piece into a small ball between the palms of the hands. Lightly flour the pastry board and rolling pin and roll the balls out into thin, circular pancakes about 5 in in diameter.

Place a skillet over heat and brush it with sesame seed oil. Add one pancake and cook briefly on both sides; if brown spots appear, the pancake is overcooked.

Continue until all the pancakes are cooked. Fold into triangles once they are cooked and wrap in a clean linen cloth, until they are served. This quantity will make 12 servings.

PASTA

The first and most important rule is to cook pasta in plenty of water—at least 4¼ cups for every 4 oz pasta—in a large saucepan. Add 1 dessertspoon of salt to every 4½ cups water. Pour the pasta into the water when it begins to boil. Only filled pasta (ravioli, tortellini, etc.) is added just before the water reaches boiling point to avoid them bursting open. When cooking fresh pasta or lasagne add 1–2 tablespoons of olive oil to the water to prevent the pasta sticking together. Stir the pasta as soon as you pour it into the saucepan, then stir frequently during cooking. For the best results (and evenly cooked pasta) the water should boil neither too vigorously nor too slowly, but over moderate heat. This is particularly important for fresh and filled pasta. Do not cover the saucepan while the pasta is cooking.

Drain the pasta when it is *al dente* (tender but still with a little "bite"). Remember that it will continue to cook for a couple of minutes after it is turned into the colander. Filled pasta, gnocchi and freshly made lasagne should be lifted out of the water with a large slotted spoon or ladle as soon as they rise to the surface. Dried pasta and less fragile fresh pasta can be poured straight into the colander. Drain the pasta well if you are serving it straight into individual dishes. Leave a little of the cooking water with it if you are dressing it with a sauce in a large serving tureen or if it is returned to the skillet for a few minutes. If you want to keep and reuse cooked pasta later, drain it when it is *al dente* and submerge in cold water for at least three minutes to stop further cooking. To reheat it, plunge it into boiling water for a couple of minutes, then drain well. The classic way to cook spaghetti is to keep it whole and not break it into shorter lengths. Place the spaghetti in the boiling water and push slowly as the pasta softens until it is completely submerged. Stir.

For perfect success it is important to match the right kind of pasta with the most suitable sauce. As a general rule fresh pasta marries well with lighter, more delicate flavors, such as sauces made with spinach, butter, cream, ham, mushrooms or tomatoes. Dried pasta is better suited to more pronounced flavors and more piquant ingredients, such as garlic, chili pepper, game, pork and the richer meat sauces.

How to prepare homemade pasta

Fresh pasta
Sift the flour into a mound on a work surface or marble top and make a well in the center. Pour the whole eggs one at a time (1 egg for every ¾ cup + 3 tbsp flour) into the well, add salt and beat in the eggs with a fork. Continue to beat with a fork until the mixture can be worked by hand. Knead the dough for about 10 minutes by hand. When the dough is smooth and elastic roll out on a floured work surface to the desired thickness.

Fresh spinach pasta
Use 3½ oz spinach for every ¾ cup + 3 tbsp flour. Cook the spinach in the minimum of boiling salted water for 5–10 minutes or until tender. Drain well and blend in a blender. Pour into the well in the center after the beaten eggs. Mix together and knead as illustrated opposite.

Tagliatelle, fettuccine, tagliolini and pappardelle
Roll out a thin sheet of pasta and cut into strips 10–12 in wide. Roll each strip over on itself three or four times. Using a very sharp knife cut into smaller strips, ⅛, ¼, ⅓, ¾ in wide depending on whether you are making tagliolini, tagliatelle, fettuccine or pappardelle. Spread the pasta out on a clean cloth to unravel and dry the strips.

Lasagne
To make squares of lasagne, roll out a sheet of pasta and cut into 5-in squares. Place the lasagne one at a time in a large saucepan of boiling salted water with 1 tbsp olive oil to prevent them sticking. Cook for 3–5 minutes; drain when *al dente* and spread out to dry on a clean cloth. Place a layer of lasagne in the bottom of a buttered ovenproof baking pan. Cover with the filling and continue layering with pasta and filling until all the ingredients are used up. Finish with a layer of pasta and place a few flakes of butter on top.

Cannelloni
Proceed as for lasagne as far as cooking.

Place a spoonful of filling in the center of each square of pasta. Roll up into cannelloni. Arrange in a buttered ovenproof baking dish and cover with sauce.

Filled pasta
To make small filled pasta, roll out half the dough into a thin sheet and place small balls of filling on top at regular intervals of about 2 in. Brush around the filling with a pastry brush dipped in water or egg white. Cover with the second sheet of pasta. Press firmly round the edges of the filling to seal. Cut out small squares or circles of filled pasta using a pastry wheel or serrated pasta cutters.

PASTRY BAG & DECORATING TIPS
When decorating cakes and desserts with whipped cream, icing or butter cream, use a pastry bag and an assortment of decorating tips. Each tip produces a different patterned effect:

Plain tip has a small round hole for making drops, blobs, dots and for writing and drawing.
Star or pointed tip is used to make stars, rosettes and shells.
Petal tip lets you make decorative scrolls, ribbons and delicate flower designs.
Large drop tip has a large round hole for making large drops, blobs, dots, writing, and drawing.
Flower tip is used to make small flowers.
Leaf tip makes delicate leaf and flower designs.

PASTRY CREAM
6 egg yolks
1¼ cups confectioner's sugar
½ cup all-purpose flour
2¼ cups milk
1 tsp vanilla extract or a small piece of lemon peel
1 tbsp butter or margarine

In a medium bowl, beat egg yolks and sugar until pale. While continuing to beat, gradually sift in the flour. Gradually add the milk. Place over low heat. Add the vanilla or lemon peel. Cook, stirring constantly, until the mixture has thickened to custard consistency (about 15 minutes). Remove from the heat. Discard lemon peel. Melt butter or margarine on the surface of the pastry cream to prevent a skin from forming while it cools. Makes about 3 cups.

Variations

Zabaglione pastry cream
Add 2–3 tablespoons dry Marsala.

Chocolate pastry cream
Add 2 oz grated chocolate or unsweetened cocoa powder.

PESTO SAUCE
¼ cup pine nuts
2 oz fresh basil leaves
salt
2 cloves garlic
1 tbsp grated Parmesan
1 tbsp grated Pecorino cheese
scant 1 cup olive oil

Lightly toast the pine nuts in a hot oven, 400°F. Rinse and dry the basil leaves. Place in a mortar or blender, add salt, garlic and the pine nuts and pound or blend to a paste. Add the cheeses gradually. When the paste is smooth, transfer to a bowl and gradually stir in the olive oil using a wooden spoon. Serve with pasta.

PILAF RICE
1 onion
1 tbsp oil
½ cup butter
1½ cups long-grain rice
salt and pepper
1 pint stock

Chop a medium onion finely and sauté very gently in an ovenproof casserole dish in the oil and ¼ cup of butter until the onion is soft but not brown. Sprinkle in the rice and stir over high heat for 2 minutes. Season with a little salt and freshly ground pepper. Stir in the hot stock and bring to a boil. Cover the casserole dish and place in a preheated oven at 350°F for 20–25 minutes. Transfer to a heated serving dish, stir in the remaining butter and serve.

PLAIN BOILED RICE
2 quarts water
salt
1 cup long-grain rice

Bring the water to a boil in a large saucepan; add salt then sprinkle in the rice. Boil for 12–15 minutes or until the rice is just tender. Drain and rinse well. Spread the rice on a clean dish towel on a large cookie sheet. Place in the oven, preheated to 350°F, for 10 minutes, for the rice to dry.

PRESERVES
Preserve describes several different kinds of products:

Jelly
Clear fruit juice is cooked with sugar to make a gel. Add pectin to juice that doesn't contain enough natural pectin to gel. Jelly will hold its shape when turned out of a mold.

Jam
Whole or chopped fruit is cooked with sugar. It is soft enough to spread easily.

Preserve
Whole or large pieces of fruit are suspended in a lightly gelled syrup.

Conserve
Conserve is similar to jam with nuts and raisins added. Chutneys may be conserves with onion, peppers and spices added.

Pickles
This refers to vegetables preserved in brine, oil or vinegar and to spicy chutneys made from fruits and vegetables with added garlic, onion, pepper, mustard and vinegar.

PUFF PASTRY
2¾ cups flour
1 tsp salt
scant 1 cup water
½ cup + 2 tbsp butter

Sift the flour and salt into a large bowl. Add the water gradually and mix to form a smooth dough. Wrap in a clean cloth and place in the refrigerator for 30 minutes. Shape the butter into a rectangle. Roll out the dough into an 8-inch square. Place the butter in the middle and fold over the edges of the dough to enclose it. Sprinkle lightly with flour and roll out into a ½-inch rectangle, 20 × 8 in. Fold into three, folding the bottom third up and the top third down. Roll out into a rectangle the same size as before. Make a quarter turn and fold the dough in three again. Wrap in wax paper and place in the refrigerator for 1 hour. Repeat the rolling out and folding operations twice more. Place the dough in the refrigerator for another hour. Remove from the refrigerator 1 hour before the dough is required.

RÉMOULADE SAUCE
1¾ cups mayonnaise (*q.v.*)
1 tsp mustard
1 tsp capers
1 tsp gherkins
½ tsp chopped basil
½ tsp chopped parsley
1 tsp anchovy paste

Mix together the mayonnaise and mustard. Stir well and add the chopped capers, gherkins, basil, and parsley. When these ingredients are well blended, stir in the anchovy paste and mix well.

SPONGE CAKE
6 eggs, separated
¾ cup sugar
1½ cups cake flour, sifted
¼ tsp vanilla extract

Preheat oven to 325°F. Grease and lightly flour an 8- or 10-inch springform pan. In a medium bowl, beat egg yolks with sugar and vanilla until light and fluffy. Beat egg whites until stiff but not dry; fold carefully into egg mixture. Fold in flour. Pour batter into prepared pan. Bake 10-inch cake 40 minutes or 8-inch cake 45 minutes or until cake tests done. An 8-inch cake can be split into 3 layers. A 10-inch cake can be split into 2 layers. Makes 1 (8- or 10-inch) cake.

SUGAR SYRUPS & CANDIES

Test	Description	Temperature
Veil	Sugar is dissolved. Syrup runs from spoon in a sheet.	200–215°F (95–100°C)
Thread	Dropped from a spoon, syrup spins a 2-inch thread.	230–234°F (110–112°C)
Soft ball Fondant Fudge Penuche	Dropped in very cold water, syrup forms a soft ball that flattens slightly when removed from water. When kneaded, it becomes soft and pliable.	234–240°F (112–116°C)
Firm ball	Dropped in very cold water, syrup forms a firm ball that does not flatten.	244–248°F (118–120°C)
Hard ball Divinity	Dropped in very cold water, syrup forms a hard ball.	250–266°F (121–130°C)
Soft crack Butter-scotch Taffy	Dropped in very cold water, syrup separates into a hard but not brittle thread.	270–290°F (132–143°C)
Hard Crack Brittle	Dropped in very cold water, syrup separates into a hard, brittle thread.	300–310°F (149–154°C)
Caramel-ized sugar	Syrup turns dark golden, but will turn black at 350°F (175°C)	310–338°F (155–170°C)

Caramel is the last stage reached when boiling a sugar syrup. The syrup turns a deep golden brown just before it burns. Caramel is used as a flavoring for desserts, syrups and sauces. Use a small heavy saucepan or skillet with a flat bottom to caramelize sugar. The heavy saucepan ensures even cooking. In a light pan, it will burn in some spots before it browns in others.

If caramelized sugar is used as a flavoring for custard (as with Crème Caramel, for example) after baking, cool completely, then refrigerate at least 2 hours. This lets the caramel soften and take moisture from the custard. When it is turned out, the caramel syrup will come out with the custard. If turned out immediately after cooking, the caramel is still hard and will remain in the mold.

There are two methods of making caramelized sugar. In one, the sugar is melted and browned. In the other, sugar and water are cooked until browned.

To make the first, stirring carefully, heat ⅓ to ½ cup granulated sugar over medium heat until the sugar melts and turns golden brown. As the caramelized sugar cools, it becomes hard, so use immediately. Pour into a mold, tipping to distribute evenly. Or pour boiling water, a little at a time, into the melted, browned sugar to make a syrup. Stir until smooth and all of caramel is dissolved.

Caramel syrup is easily made by boiling ½ cup granulated sugar and ¼ cup water until sugar dissolves. Without stirring, continue boiling until mixture is caramelized. Stirring may cause the syrup to crystallize before it browns. Caramel syrup changes color fast, so watch it carefully. When lightly browned, it is mild and sweet. The darker it becomes, the richer the caramel flavor—unless it burns. Then it is bitter and not usable. Remove from the heat from time to time to control the cooking. When the color is deep golden, dip the base of the pan in cold water to stop cooking immediately. Use to drizzle over fruit, or use in recipes calling for caramelized sugar or caramel syrup.

Liqueur sugar syrup
1½ cups sugar
2 cups water
1 cup liqueur of your choice

In a medium saucepan, combine sugar and water. Stir over medium heat until sugar dissolves. Stir in liqueur. Makes about 3 cups.

SWEET SHORTCRUST PASTRY
1¾ cups all-purpose flour
½ cup sugar
½ tsp salt
½ cup butter
2 eggs, slightly beaten
1 tsp grated lemon peel or ⅛ tsp vanilla extract

This sweet shortcrust pastry is the basic recipe on which there are several variations. Cocoa powder, ground almonds or hazelnuts can be added. Shortcrust pastry should be prepared as quickly as possible, otherwise it crumbles when rolled out.

In a medium bowl, combine flour, sugar and salt. Make a well in center. Work in butter. Add eggs and lemon peel or vanilla. Blend all ingredients together until a smooth ball of pastry is formed. Press pastry in bottom and side of pan. Or, refrigerate for 30 minutes. Then roll pastry to desired size. Bake at 450°F 10 to 12 minutes. Bake tarts or tartlets at 375°F 15 to 20 minutes or until golden brown. The quantities given here are sufficient for a 9-inch flan pan; a 7-inch pie pan, 8 (3½-inch) tarts or 20 tartlets.

TARTAR SAUCE

2 hard-boiled egg yolks
1¾ cups oil
salt and pepper
1 tbsp finely chopped chives
1 tbsp mayonnaise
1 tsp vinegar

Finely sieve the egg yolks. Add the oil in a thin stream, stirring constantly. Season with salt and pepper. Add the chives, mayonnaise, and vinegar and stir well until the sauce is smooth.

TESTING FOR DONENESS

Most desserts are baked a specific amount of time. However, due to variance in oven temperature, it is always wise to test the product to see if it is done. The following are some of the tests that can be made:

Custard
Insert a knife in the center or between the center and side of the dish. If the knife comes out clean—does not have any custard on it—the custard is done. This test is used for individual custards and custard pies.

Bread
Most breads can be tested for doneness by tapping the top with your fingertips. If it sounds hollow, the bread is done. Or, remove the bread from the pan or baking sheet and tap the bottom with your fingertips. If the loaf sounds hollow, it is done.

Quick breads and breads containing nuts or fruit
These are tested by inserting a wooden pick near the center of the loaf where it will not puncture any fruit or nuts. If it comes out clean and dry, the bread is done. If the bottom of the bread is not as browned as you desire, place the loaf directly on the oven rack. Bake about 5 minutes or to desired brownness.

Cake
Bake minimum time if a range is given before testing doneness. To test most cakes, insert a wooden pick near the center. If the pick comes out clean and dry, the cake is done. If the cake layer is thin, as in a *jelly roll*, press the top with your fingertips. If the surface springs back, the cake is done. At any time, if the cake does not test done, return it to the oven for another 5 to 10

minutes. When done, the cake should pull away from the side of the pan.

TOMATO SAUCE

14 oz ripe tomatoes
salt
3 tbsp olive oil
1 tbsp chopped fresh basil

Skin the tomatoes (covering them with boiling water for a few minutes to loosen the skin), remove the seeds and chop the flesh into small pieces. Place in a skillet with salt to taste and 1 tbsp olive oil and cook for 6 minutes. Sieve the cooked tomatoes. Pour the sauce back into the skillet, add the remaining oil and the basil and cook for 1 minute.

VANILLA

When a recipe calls for vanilla, it generally means pure vanilla extract that is obtained from the vanilla plant, a member of the orchid family.

Artificial vanilla, which is produced chemically, is widely available but has a slightly bitter taste.

Vanilla sugar
Vanilla sugar is available in supermarkets and specialty stores. But you can easily make your own. In a 1-pint jar, combine 1½ cups granulated sugar and 1 vanilla bean. Cover tightly. Let stand 1 or 2 weeks before using. Shake jar periodically. As the flavored sugar is used, add more sugar.

YEAST DOUGHS

Almost any dough can be prepared with yeast, from brioche dough to pizza bases to cakes. For desserts and sweet breads, use low-gluten or all-purpose flour. This will give you a more tender product.

Sugar adds flavor and tenderness to bread, helps to brown the crust and gives a delicate texture. It also helps yeast breads to rise faster.

Salt improves the flavor of yeast doughs. If no salt or less than the recommended amount is used, the flavor will be bland and the dough may rise too quickly. Too much salt will hinder the rising of the dough and may spoil the texture of the final result.

Use warm liquid—usually water, milk or fruit juices. If the recipe includes butter or eggs, the amount of liquid required is less. Sometimes no additional liquid is needed.

Always proof yeast. Combine proofed yeast with other ingredients as the recipe directs. Beat with an electric mixer or by hand. This initial beating shortens kneading time.

Kneading is important because it develops the gluten strands, making a fine-textured bread. To knead, place the dough on a lightly floured surface. With lightly floured hands, pick up the dough edge on the side away from you. Fold it

toward you. Press down firmly on the dough with the heels of your hands while gently pushing away from you. Turn the dough ¼ turn. Again pick up the dough on the side away from you, fold it over and press down firmly while pushing away from you. Repeat this action for about 10 minutes until the dough is smooth and elastic.

After kneading, place the dough in a clean, greased bowl. Cover and let rise in a warm place, free from drafts, until doubled in bulk. This may be done by placing the bowl of dough inside another bowl half-full of warm water or placing the dough in an unheated oven. Place a pan of hot water on the shelf below the dough.

Punch down the dough and shape as directed in the recipe. Again, let rise until doubled in bulk. Bake as directed.

If you are making a batter bread, add only enough flour to the yeast mixture to make a stiff batter. Beat well to develop the gluten. Cover and let rise in a warm place, such as over a pan of warm water. Stir down and turn into a prepared pan. Let rise again; bake as directed.

ZABAGLIONE CREAM

3 egg yolks
½ cup confectioner's sugar
¼ cup Marsala or white wine
1¼ cups whipping cream

In a medium glass bowl, beat egg yolks and sugar until pale. Beat in wine, 1 tablespoon at a time. Place bowl in a *bain marie* over low heat. Beat with a whisk until mixture is light and fluffy. Cool, stirring occasionally. Beat whipping cream until stiff. Carefully fold into cooked mixture. Makes about 4 cups.

Index

Acknowledgment

The publishers thank the following for kindly supplying photographic material:
Emilio Fabio Simion, Adriano Brusaferri, Giuseppe Losito, Fredi Marcarini,
Shogakukan Publishing Co. Ltd., Tokyo.